THE SPECIAL EDUCATION AUDIT HANDBOOK

DONALD F. WEINSTEIN, Ph.D.

President, Educational Services Associates, Inc.

TECHNOMIC
PUBLISHING CO., INC.
LANCASTER · BASEL

HOW TO ORDER THIS BOOK

BY PHONE: 800-233-9936 or 717-291-5609, 8AM–5PM Eastern Time

BY FAX: 717-295-4538

BY MAIL: Order Department
Technomic Publishing Company, Inc.
851 New Holland Avenue, Box 3535
Lancaster, PA 17604, U.S.A.

BY CREDIT CARD: American Express, VISA, MasterCard

BY WWW SITE: http://www.techpub.com

PERMISSION TO PHOTOCOPY–POLICY STATEMENT

To my youngest son Erick Harris Weinstein,
who has the patience and perseverance of both his paternal and maternal grandfathers
for whom he was named and a little more.
On a good day, I can get a hug, a kiss, and a smile from him,
and that makes my day a lot brighter and my blood a lot warmer.

The Special Education Audit Handbook
a **TECHNOMIC** ⓡ publication

Published in the Western Hemisphere by
Technomic Publishing Company, Inc.
851 New Holland Avenue, Box 3535
Lancaster, Pennsylvania 17604 U.S.A.

Distributed in the Rest of the World by
Technomic Publishing AG
Missionsstrasse 44
CH-4055 Basel, Switzerland

Printed in the United States of America
10 9 8 7 6 5 4 3 2 1

Main entry under title:
The Special Education Audit Handbook

A Technomic Publishing Company book
Bibliography: p.
Includes index p. 127

Library of Congress Catalog Card No. 96-61123
ISBN No. 1-56676-463-7

Table of Contents

Acknowledgements   xi

Introduction   xiii

1. **DEMYSTIFYING SPECIAL EDUCATION FOR NEW AND OLD SUPERINTENDENTS, ASSISTANT SUPERINTENDENTS, AND PRINCIPALS WHO HAVE HAD LIMITED EXPERIENCE WITH SPECIAL EDUCATION** **1**

    Aim   1

    Introduction   1

    Acronyms and Terms   1

    Time Lines   1

    Referrals   3

    Summary   3

    Reference   3

2. **GATHERING INFORMATION: TOOLS AND COMMITTEE** **5**

    Aim   5

    Instruments, Boilerplates, and Illustrations   5

       Illustration: Method to Determine Number of People to Survey   6

    Special Education Task Force   21

3. **QUICK OVERVIEW OF YOUR SPECIAL EDUCATION PROGRAM** **23**

    Aim   23

    Introduction   23

    Illustration: Percent of Classified Students   23

    Boilerplate: Percent of Classified Students   24

    Illustration: Number of Special Education Teachers   25

    Summary   26

4. **THE FIRST STEPS IN AN AUDIT OF THE REFERRAL PROCESS** **27**

    Aim   27

    Profile of Classroom Teachers Who Refer Students for Evaluation
       for Special Education .   27

    Illustration: Profile of Classroom Teachers Who Had Referred Students
       for Evaluation for Placement in Special Education   28

    Illustration: Number of Students Referred for Placement   29

    Boilerplate: Transfer Students   29

Locally Written Criteria   29

Illustration: Anecdotal Comments about Locally Written Criteria for
    Classification of Students   30

Problems/Difficulties That Trigger Referrals   30

Steps to Remediate Problems   31

Purpose for Referrals   31

Role of Special Education Personnel in the Referral Process   31

Role of the Building Administrator in Teachers' Referrals of Students   32

Referrals by Gender   33

Boilerplate: Presentation of Information by Gender   33

Referrals by Student's Family Status   35

Boilerplate: Presentation of Information by Family Status   35

Summary   37

**5. SIX STEPS TO REDUCE THE NUMBER OF REFERRALS
OF STUDENTS EVENTUALLY CLASSIFIED LEARNING DISABLED** **39**

Aim   39

Referrals of Students Who Were Eventually Classified Learning Disabled   39

Referrals by Gender   40

    Illustration: Referral of Students Eventually Classified LD by Gender   40

Step 1 to Reduce the Size of the Student Pool   41

    Terms Used to Refer Students   41

    *Illustration: "Academic" Terms Used to Describe Students
        Who Eventually Are Classified LD*   41

Step 2 to Reduce the Size of the Student Pool   42

    *School Psychologists and the Ability to Differentiate Low-Achieving
        Students from Learning Disabled Students*   42

    Competency of School Psychologists   43

Step 3 to Reduce the Size of the Student Pool   43

    Intelligence Range: Low Ability Students and LD Classification   43

Step 4 to Reduce the Size of the Student Pool   44

    Referrals by Grade Level: Is the Educational Program Appropriate?   44

Step 5 to Reduce the Size of the Student Pool   46

    Referrals by Student's Family Status   46

Step 6 to Reduce the Size of the Student Pool   46

Summary   46

References   47

**6. FOUR STEPS TO REDUCE THE NUMBER OF REFERRALS OF
STUDENTS EVENTUALLY CLASSIFIED SPEECH IMPAIRED** **49**

Aim   49

Definition of Speech Impaired   49

Justifications Given for the Numbers of Students Identified Speech Impaired   49

Doubts Raised about Speech and Language Referrals   50

Step 1 to Reduce the Size of the Student Pool   50

    Referrals by Gender   51

    Illustration: Referral of Students Eventually Classified SI by Gender   51

    Terms Used by Gender   51

Step 2 to Reduce the Size of the Student Pool   51

    Examples of Terms and Phrases Used to Refer Students   51

Step 3 to Reduce the Size of the Student Pool   53
   Nonspeech and Language Reasons Given for Students That Were
      Eventually Classified SI   53
   Referral of Students Eventually Classified SI by Grade Level   53
Step 4 to Reduce the Size of the Student Pool   53
   Referrals by Students' Intelligence Range   54
   Referrals by Student's Family Status   54
Summary   54

**7. SIX STEPS TO REDUCE THE NUMBER OF REFERRALS
OF STUDENTS EVENTUALLY CLASSIFIED
EMOTIONALLY DISTURBED** **57**

Aim   57
Referrals of Students Who Were Eventually Classified Emotionally Disturbed   57
Definition of Emotionally Disturbed   58
Step 1 to Reduce the Size of the Student Pool   58
   Referrals by Gender   58
   Illustration: Referral of Students Eventually Classified ED by Gender   58
Step 2 to Reduce the Size of the Student Pool   59
   Terms Used to Refer Students   59
   Examples of Terms and Phrases Used to Refer Students   59
Step 3 to Reduce the Size of the Student Pool   61
   Referral of Students by Grade Level   61
Step 4 to Reduce the Size of the Student Pool   61
   Referrals by Students' Intelligence Range   61
Step 5 to Reduce the Size of the Student Pool   63
   Referrals by Students' Family Status   63
Step 6 to Reduce the Size of the Student Pool   63
Summary   63

8. THE COMMITTEE ON SPECIAL EDUCATION **65**

Aim   65
Overview of Concerns   65
Composition of the Committee of Special Education   65
Number of CSEs   65
Step 1 to Reduce the Size of the Student Pool   66
   Attendance at CSE Meetings   66
   Principals   66
Step 2 to Reduce the Size of the Student Pool   66
   The Classification Process   66
   Role of the Psychologists   67
   Weight of Assessment   68
   Reports and Research Regarding Assessment   68
Step 3 to Reduce the Size of the Student Pool   69
   Role of the Special Education Director   69
   Parent Reaction to CSE   69
Step 4 to Reduce the Size of the Student Pool   70
   Effective or Ineffective Gatekeeper   70
Step 5 to Reduce the Size of the Student Pool   71
Summary   71
References   71

9. MINORITY STUDENTS **73**

  Aim   73

  The Ethnic-Racial Issue in Special Education   73

  Four General Findings Regarding Race   73

  Referrals by Race and Ethnic Group   74

  District 1   74
    Demographics   74
    African American   74
    African American Females   75
    Terms/Phrases Used in Referrals by Racial/Ethnic Group by Gender   75
  District 2   78
    Referrals by Gender   78
    Terms/Phrases Used in Referrals by Gender   78
    Classification of African American Students   79
    African American Females   79
    Latinos   79
  Summary   83

**10. SUPERVISION OF SPECIAL EDUCATION PERSONNEL:
MORE EFFECTIVE AND EFFICIENT USE OF TEACHING
ASSISTANTS, PSYCHOLOGISTS, SOCIAL WORKERS,
AND LD TEACHER-CONSULTANTS** **85**

  Aim   85

  Introduction   85

  Organizational Structure of Special Education   85
    Background   85
    Responsibilities of Directors of Special Education   85
    *The Views of Special Education Teachers on Supervision by Principals
      and Special Education Directors*   86
    Supervision of Special Education Teachers   86
    *Special Education Teachers' Perceptions of the Roles of Principals in the
      Supervision of Special Education*   86
    Views of Principals on Their Role in Supervising Special Education Teachers   87
    Steps for Principals to Take to Improve Supervision of Special Education Teachers   88
    Director of Special Education   88
    *Special Education Teachers' Perceptions of the Roles of the Directors of Special
      Education in the Supervision of Special Education*   89
    Principals' Perceptions of the Role of the Directors of Special Education   89
    Steps for Principals to Take to Improve Supervision of Special Education Teachers   89
    Supervision of Support Personnel   90
    Teaching Assistants   90
    Anecdotal Comments by Special Education Teachers about Teaching Assistants   90
    Anecdotal Comments by Principals about Teaching Assistants   91
    The Actual Use of Teaching Assistants   91
    *Steps for Directors of Special Education to Take to Improve the Supervision
      of Special Education Teaching Assistants*   92
    Psychologists, Social Workers, and Learning Disabilities Teacher-Consultants   92
    *Steps for Directors of Special Education to Take to Improve the Supervision
      of Psychologists, Social Workers, and LD Teacher-Consultants*   93
  Summary   93

11. SUPERVISION OF THE SPECIAL EDUCATION CURRICULUM **95**

  Aim   95

Introduction   95

Social Studies Audits   96

Social Studies Understandings/Objectives   97
   Illustration from District 3   97
   Illustration from District 4   98
   Illustrations from District 5   98

Steps You Can Take to Improve Your Special Education Curriculum   99

Curriculum Mapping   99
   Illustration: Alignment between General Health Program and the Special Education Health Program by Grade Level   100
   Illustration: Alignment between General High School English, Social Studies, Science, and Mathematics Programs and the Special Education Programs   101

Parents   101

Summary   101

12. **ACCOUNTABILITY OF SPECIAL EDUCATION PROGRAMS: LENGTH OF TIME STUDENTS ARE CLASSIFIED, PULL-OUT PROGRAMS, AND PLACEMENT OF MINORITY STUDENTS** **103**

Aim   103

Introduction   103

First Step to Downsize the Number of Classified Students by Categories   103

Second Step to Downsize the Number of Classified Students by Categories   104

Third Step to Downsize the Number of Classified Students by Categories   105

Fourth Step to Downsize the Number of Classified Students by Categories   105
   Mainstreaming   105
   Criteria Used to Mainstream Students   106
   Learning Disabled   106
   Length of Time Students Are Classified LD by Ethnicity/Race   107
   Insights Provided by Psychologists about the Length of Time That Students Are Classified LD   107
   LD Students Who Receive Regular Classroom Instruction and Related Services or Resource Room or Part-Time Special Class Programs   108
   Parents' Views on Pull-Out Programs   109
   Consultant Models   109
   LD Students in Pull-Out Programs: An Example   109
   Number of LD Teachers   109
   Speech Impaired   110
   Length of Time Students Are Classified SI by Ethnicity/Race   110
   SI Students Who Receive Regular Classroom Instruction and Related Services or Resource Room or Part-Time Special Class Programs   110
   Number of SI Teachers   111
   Criticisms of Pull-Out Speech Therapy Programs   111
   Emotionally Disturbed   112
   Length of Time Students Are Classified ED by Ethnicity/Race   112
   ED Students Who Receive Regular Classroom Instruction and Related Services or Resource Room or Part-Time Special Class Programs and ED Students Enrolled in Special Public Schools or Nonschool Facilities   112
   ED Students in Pull-Out Programs: An Example   113
   Number of ED Teachers   114

Fifth Step to Downsize the Number of Classified Students by Categories   114
   Minority Students   114

Summary   114

13. THE DECLASSIFICATION PROCESS **117**

   Aim   117

   Introduction   117

   Bottleneck 1: Lack of Written Criteria for Declassification   118

     Director of Special Education   118

     Declassification of SI Students   118

     Declassification of LD Students   118

     State Criteria and/or a 50% Discrepancy   118

     Test and Observation   119

     Success in Mainstreamed Classes without the Need of Support Services   119

     Declassification of ED Students   119

     Actual Reasons for Declassification of Students   120

     Roles of Principals in the Declassification Process   120

     Role of Special Education Personnel in the Declassification Process   120

     Steps to Build Equity, Objectivity, and Accountability into the
       Declassification Process   121

   Bottleneck 2: Concerns/Fears about Schoolwide Test Scores   121

     Illustration: Declassification of Students by Grade   121

   Bottleneck 3: Gender and Ethnic/Racial Bias   121

     Illustration: Demographics of Declassified Students   121

     Declassification of Minority Students   121

   Summary   123

14. CONCLUSION **125**

Index   127

About the Author   129

Acknowledgements

ALTHOUGH this book is based on my experiences with special education audits, I am indebted to former and present educational leaders in school districts, colleges/universities, state education departments, and professional organizations. Specifically, I am indebted to the superintendents and directors of special education and teachers in districts in which I have designed, planned, and implemented audits. I owe a special thanks to Dr. H. William Heller, Dean, University of Southern Florida, St. Petersburg, Florida. Although I have spoken with Dr. Heller on numerous occasions, I have never met him. Yet he has always been gracious with his time as he edited my articles for publication in *Case in Point*. His editorial suggestions always improved my articles. Dr. Heller's behavior typifies, for me, the highest level of professional responsibility exhibited by a Dean.

I am indebted to four people over the years for their friendship, encouragement, and support. These people include Mrs. Joan Milowe, Associate, New York State Education Department; Mr. Edward Porter, Superintendent and Deputy Director, National Center on Education and the Economy; and Dr. Arnold Raisner, Superintendent, New York City and Professor, C.W. Post College, New York. However, I am especially indebted to Dr. Pierre Woog, Dean and Professor, Adelphi University, New York, whose intellectual questions, insights, and suggestions helped me to focus the book.

The influence that my contact with Robert Oppenheim, business consultant, has had on me cannot be minimized. He helped to unleash my productive and creative juices. There were many other people who have helped me over the years, including Edward T. Lalor, Assistant Commissioner, New York State Education Department, Dr. Bruce Crowder, Dean Helen Greene, Dean Walter M. Matthews, Associate Dean Laura Sqroi, Professor Joe Trippi, and Ms. Candie Countryman.

This book owes a great deal to three important people in my life—my oldest son Jeffrey Mark Weinstein, my middle son Robert Scott Weinstein, and Anne Jassie Weinstein, my daughter-in-law. They have shared an interest in my work.

Finally and importantly, there is Dale McInerney. Dale has done all the tasks that one does as an act of devotion and more. She read, reacted to, proofed, corrected, and took pride in the manuscript. I bounced ideas off of her, and I valued her insights, especially into the concerns of teachers. But more than anything else she provided me with a warm and loving home and worked with me to make our lives work.

Introduction

THE old blues guitarist Memphis Slim wailed, "Everybody wants to get to heaven but nobody wants to die." Well, everybody wants to downsize programs, curtail mushrooming costs, deliver needed services, and still ensure the equity and excellence of special education programs. In order to do that, a lot of nitty gritty work is required, and an honest evaluation of the referral, classification, and declassification processes is essential. But this means a change in your role if you are a superintendent, assistant superintendent, or principal. In the past, you were expected to behave like a corpse at an Irish wake when the people who managed and operated special education spoke on the subject; that is, everyone expected you to be present, but nobody expected you to have much to say. Well, those days have changed, especially as the number of classified students increases, classified student outcomes are questioned, and dollars become scarce.

Whether you are a superintendent, assistant superintendent, principal, or director of special education, you need to demonstrate that all aspects of the special education program are well administered and worth every penny spent on it. Or you need to reform the program. In order to make that judgement, you need hard data and anecdotal information about the management and operation of the special education program. Specifically, you need to know whether the prereferral, referral, classification, mainstreaming, and declassification processes are objective, equitable, and effective. When the entrance and exiting processes are well managed and operated, only students that truly need services are classified, students are classified properly, special education costs are reduced, and the integrity of the program is enhanced.

The step-by-step audit spelled out in this book shows you how to gather, organize, analyze and evaluate information about the effectiveness and efficiency of the management and operation of your special education program. It provides you with surveys and charts that you can use to implement your own audit. This process has been used in districts with as few as 100 classified students and districts that had over 2500 classified students. Moreover, this book provides you with cutting edge information about the actual management and operation of special education programs as a means to illustrate various findings from an audit.

If you follow the process spelled out in this book, you will have gathered an album of snapshots that will help you determine whether the management and operation of the special education program is effective and efficient and in line with the spirit and letter of the law. You will be able to identify and take steps to cut fat, eliminate bottlenecks and increase the productivity of the special education program. You will be able to reduce costs, downsize the program, and ensure the equity, objectivity, and effectiveness of the special education program. Specifically, this text will help you determine

- referral patterns by school, grade, gender, race/ethnicity, socioeconomic and family status
- whether academic, behavior, speech and hearing or other reasons were the rationale for the referrals and whether specific terms were used to refer specific students by gender, socioeconomic and/or racial/ethnic groups and family structure for evaluation for special education
- the degree to which principals, psychologists, committee on special education members (CSE), and classroom teachers were knowledgeable about criteria for classification, mainstreaming, and declassification of students
- the linkage between the general curriculum and the curriculum for self-contained special education classes
- roles played by teaching assistants and/or aides in the delivery of programs
- roles played by classroom teachers, psychologists, special education teachers, and

administrators in the referral, classification, and declassification process
- reasons for declassification and profiles of declassified students

Remember, there is a great deal of skepticism about the integrity of the referral, classification, and declassification components of special education programs. There is concern that the structure and delivery of regular classroom instruction is at cross purposes with the developmental stage of and ways young boys learn (Restak, 1979). There is suspicion about placement decisions and leeriness about the term learning disabled, a term so vague that more than 80% of students could be classified as learning disabled by the definitions used (Ysseldyke, Algozzine, Rickey, and Graden, 1982; Ysseldyke, Algozzine, Shinn, and McGue, 1982; Gartner and Lipsky, 1987). At least 50% of learning disabled students are slow learners, children from second-language backgrounds, naughty in class, excessive absentees, transients, or average learners in an above-average school system (Shepard, Smith, and Vojir, 1983). There is doubt that committees on special education serve as effective gatekeepers to special education (Garcia and Ortiz, 1988). There is mistrust about the competency and integrity of school psychologists in recommending classifications (Figueroa, 1991). There is apprehension about the integrity of academic programs for self-contained special education students. And there is anxiety that pull-out programs such as LD resource room, speech therapy, and counseling hinder children from learning the information and skills needed to succeed in school (Creaghead, 1990). All these issue impact on the size, cost, deliver, equity, objectivity, and effectiveness of special education programs.

This book provides a process to make informed judgments about all aspects of the special education program based on facts rather than pressure. Oftentimes, the facts provide you with a roadmap of how to downsize your special education program, reduce costs, and yet improve the delivery of the special education program surgically. Also, illustrations represent actual findings from audits and, therefore, provide you with a wealth of practical and usable information about the nuts and bolts of the management and operation of the special education program. You will have the information needed to validate the effectiveness and efficiency of the management and operation of special education and/or the specific information you need to reform components and/or all aspects of the management and operation of the program.

REFERENCES

Creaghead, N. (1990). Mutual Empowerment through Collaboration: A New Script for an Old Problem, *Best Practices in School Speech Language Pathology*, 1:109–116.

Figueroa, R. A. (1991, September). ''The Reform of Assessment Practices in Special Education: The California Experience,'' lecture sponsored by the U.S. Office of Bilingual Education.

Garcia, S. B. and Ortiz, A. A. (1988). Preventing Inappropriate Referrals of Language Minority Students to Special Education, *FOCUS: The National Clearinghouse for Bilingual Education*, 5:2–11.

Gartner, A. and Lipsky, D. K. (1987). Beyond Special Education: Toward a Quality System for All Students, *Harvard Educational Review*, 57:367–395.

Restak, R. M. (1979). The Other Difference between Boys and Girls, *Educational Leadership*, 37:232–235.

Shepard, L. A., Smith, M. L. and Vojir, C. P. (1983). Characteristics of Pupils Identified as Learning Disabled, *American Educational Research Journal*, 20:309–331.

Ysseldyke, J. E., Algozzine, B., Rickey, L. and Graden, J. (1982). Declaring Students Eligible for Learning Disability Services: Why Bother with Data, *Learning Disabilities Quarterly*, 5:37–45.

Ysseldyke, J. E., Algozzine, B., Shinn, M. and McGue, M. (1982). Similarities and Differences between Low Achievers and Students Labeled Learning Disabled, *Journal of Special Education*, 16:73–85.

Demystifying Special Education for New and Old Superintendents, Assistant Superintendents, and Principals Who Have Had Limited Experience with Special Education

AIM

THIS chapter is for people who have little knowledge of special education. The purpose of this chapter is to make sure that you are not overwhelmed by acronyms and terms tossed about by special education personnel as you take your first steps into the world of special education personnel. Nor should you be intimidated by special education time lines that require compliance by your district or uneasy when you start your audit of special education. There is a chart that lists the most frequent acronyms and terms used in special education and a chart that spells out the time lines that are most important in the daily operation of special education. Armed with this information, I hope you feel at ease as you walk step by step through the special education audit.

INTRODUCTION

Welcome to the world of special education audits. At first glance, you are likely to be overwhelmed by the alphabet soup of acronyms and terms that special education personnel use in their daily lives. Think of these terms as the handwriting used by medical doctors to write prescriptions or the collars of clergy or the stars of generals. They all are used to clarify their positions and to keep the uninitiated public at a distance, hopefully as a result of respect. More importantly, they symbolize the fact that these people know the answers whatever the questions. Once you have a pharmacology reference book or read the Bible and the thoughts of scholars or review declassified military files, you understand that there is no wizard in Oz. Well, there are no mysteries in special education—only acronyms and terms that you can learn easily.

ACRONYMS AND TERMS

Whenever I speak to your colleagues who are anxious as they take their first steps into the ocean called special education, I am reminded of an old folktale about a cat who had two mice cowering in their mousehole. The mice heard the "meow" sound of the cat, followed by the "woof" of a dog, a spitting retreat, and a thankful silence. As soon as they crept out of their shelter, the cat pounced on them, remarking as he ate them up, "I always knew it would be useful to have a second language." (DeCaro, 1995). Well, you need to know that it is easy to speak the language of special education. Chart 1.1 is a list of the most common acronyms and terms used by special education personnel. Learn these acronyms and terms, and you have taken the first step to making sense out of what appears as a mishmash of sounds. As you move through your special education audit, you may feel that you want more specific information about a handicapping condition and the treatment of that condition. In that case, you can research the needed information in books and/or have the special education personnel give you a three-credit course by asking them well thought out questions.

TIME LINES

Another area of special education that is likely to cause you concern centers on time lines for the special education process. If you are a principal, you are aware of some of the time lines that affect you right now. They probably mirror the situation faced by your colleagues in other states. For instance, in some states, you know that, if you receive a referral, you need to forward the referral to the chairperson of the committee on special education (CSE) immediately, and you know that, when the chairperson of the CSE receives a referral directly, he/she has five days to send you a copy of the referral. You know that, as principal, once you receive a referral or a copy of a referral, you have the right to request a meeting with the parents/guardians of the student to explore alternatives to special education. However, there are other time lines found in Chart 1.2 that you definitely need to comply with and ensure compliance by your special education program. But you probably

ADD	Attention deficit disorder: a disorder found in people, which interferes with their ability to sustain their attention to an activity, task, or lesson. It has a negative impact upon learning and may result in behavioral problems in some students.
ADHD	Attention deficit hyperactivity disorder: a disorder that produces hyperactivity in addition to all of the characteristics of ADD. Behavior problems may be extreme.
ADL	Activities of daily living: life skills curriculum usually prescribed for students with mental retardation.
Annual Review	The annual review is a required CSE meeting to determine whether the existing program (IEP) is appropriately meeting the student's needs. The annual review must occur once a year.
AUT	Autistic: autism is a behaviorally defined syndrome that may occur in youngsters of all levels of intelligence.
CBVH	Commission for the blind and visually handicapped
CSE	Committee on special education
CP	Cerebral palsy: a neurologically based disability that usually results in a student being classified orthopedically impaired.
Deaf	Deaf: a student who is deaf has a loss of hearing so severe that it prevents processing linguistic information through hearing.
DDSO	Developmental disabilities service office
ERSS	Educationally related support services: services provided to students prior to classification.
ED	Emotionally disturbed: such students have difficulties in school that cannot be explained by intellectual , sensory, or health factors.
FAPE	Free appropriate public education
FERPA	Family Education Rights and Privacy Act of 1974
504	Rehabilitation Act of 1973
HH	Hard of hearing: a student in this category has a hearing impairment that adversely affects his/her educational performance.
IEP	Individualized education program: federally mandated plan of service developed for every student with a disability by the committee on special education.
IHO	Impartial hearing officer: a state-approved professional who makes a determination of student service when agreement between the CSE and the parent cannot be achieved.
IQ	Intelligence quotient: measure of intelligence resulting from psychological testing.
JTPA	Job Training Partnership Act
LD	Learning disabled: these students have a psychological processing disorder that causes them to have a problem in understanding or using language, spoken or written, which manifests itself in an imperfect ability to listen, think, speak, read, write, spell, or to do mathematical calculations.
LEA	Local educational agency: the school district.
LRE	Least restrictive environment: the most normal setting possible for a student to achieve.
MH	Multiply handicapped: some students have two or more disabilities that cannot be met through a special education program designed solely for one of the disabilities.
MR	Mentally retarded: very limited intellectual ability.
OHI	Other health impaired: some students have limited strength, vitality, or alertness due to chronic or acute health problems, which adversely affects their educational performance.
OI	Orthopedically impaired: students are physically disabled and have a severe orthopedic impairment that adversely affects their educational performance.
OSES	Office for special education services
OMH	Office of mental health
OMRDD	Office of mental retardation and developmental disabilities
OT	Occupational therapists/occupational therapy
P.L. 94-142	The Education of All Handicapped Children Act
P.L. 95-561	1978 Education Amendments and Extension of P.L. 94-142
P.L. 98-199	1983 Revision and Extension of P.L. 94-142
P.L. 99-457	Preschool, Postsecondary, and Transitional Services Extension of P.L. 94-142
P.L. 100-630	1988 Technical Amendments to P.L. 94-142
P.L. 101-476	1990 The Individuals with Disabilities Education Act
PT	Physical therapist/physical therapy
RT	Recreational therapists
SI	Speech impaired: students have a communication disorder, an inability to correctly produce speech sounds, a language impairment, or a voice disorder.
SSI	Supplemental security income
Triennial Evaluation	A triennial occurs every three years. Updated information is provided through reexamining many of the areas previously tested in the initial evaluation. The purpose of this reexamination is to determine individual needs and continued eligibility for special education.
VESID	Office of vocational and educational services for individuals with disabilities
VI	Visually impaired: Students may be partially sighted or blind.

CHART 1.2 Time Lines for the Special Education Process.

Compliance Issues	Time Lines
Receipt of referral	Referrals are recieved by the chairperson of the CSE or building principal. If the referral is made to the principal, it shall be forwarded to the CSE chairperson immediately.
Recommendations to BOE by CSE	Within thirty days of the receipt of parental/guardian consent or within forty days of the date of receipt of referral, whichever period shall end earlier
BOE to provide special education programs and services	Within thirty days of receiving the CSE recommendations
Annual review	Every twelve months
Triennial evaluation	Every thirty-six months

know this. However, do you know whether your district does comply with these time lines? Are there students that should be serviced that have not, as of yet, been serviced? If your district does not comply with these time lines, do you know the reasons for this lapse? Does everyone understand that the time lines were established to ensure that youngsters who need to be in special education are provided with appropriate programs as soon as possible?

REFERRALS

In order to begin the special education audit, we need to be sure that you have a basic knowledge of referrals. First, you need to know that a referral of a student for evaluation for placement is initiated by a written request sent to the CSE or building principal. All the referral means is that the person making the referral is concerned that a youngster has learning problems that may be due to a disability. Second, a referral can be made by virtually any professional staff member in your district, the youngster's parents/guardians, an emancipated minor on his/her own behalf, and a number of state officials. Third, a thorough referral includes the reasons for believing that an educational disability ex-

ists, quantitative and qualitative assessment information, prereferral attempts made to remediate the youngster's performance, and the extent of parent involvement in the prereferral stage. Fourth, the referral is sent to either the principal or the CSE chairperson. Once these four steps are completed, the special education process unfolds.

SUMMARY

The purpose of this chapter is to make you more comfortable as you begin your special education audit. As long as you understand that there are no mysteries to special education, you can proceed with the audit with the confidence that you have when you evaluate any other program in your school/district. You are now ready to learn how to gather information to implement a practical and usable audit of your special education program.

REFERENCE

DeCaro, F. (1995). *The Folktail Cat.* New York: Barnes and Noble.

Gathering Information: Tools and Committee

AIM

THE purpose of this chapter is to spell out the information you need to gather, the instruments you need to use to obtain the information, the way to set up your database to implement an audit of your special education program, and the purpose of a special education task force (SETF). Included are six survey forms for classroom teachers, special education teachers, principals, psychologists, members of the CSE, and parents. After each survey form, there is a boilerplate that explains the way to set up a file for a database in order to automate the responses of participants. There are boilerplates for database files for students, classroom teachers, special education teachers principals, psychologists, members of the CSE, and parents.

INSTRUMENTS, BOILERPLATES, AND ILLUSTRATIONS

In order to implement an audit of the management and operation of the special education program, you need the proper tools. First, you need survey forms for classroom teachers, special education teachers, principals, psychologists, members of the CSE, and parents. Second, you need a database program to analyze hard data from either the school/district and/or the state education department and survey responses.

The database file that you create so that you can analyze information about the referral, classification, and declassification processes needs to have nineteen fields. The fields and the width of each field is standard; however, if there is information that is idiosyncratic to your school district, add another field or two. The boilerplate for referrals, classification, and declassification of students includes

Field	Width in Characters
1. Student's identification number	9
2. Student's gender	1
3. Student's school	2
4. Student's grade	2
5. Student's racial/ethnic code	1
6. Student's classification	3
7. Student's lunch/socioeconomic status	1
8. Number of biological parents with whom student resides	1
9. Student's intelligence range	2
10. Date student was referred	8
11. Date student was evaluated	8
12. Date student was classified by CSE	8
13. Date student was declassified by CSE	8
14. Number of days/months student was classified	8
15. Academic reasons for referral	10
16. Speech and hearing reasons for referral	10
17. Behavioral reasons for referral	10
18. Other reasons for referral	10
19. Reasons student left program	2

The assistant superintendent of pupil personnel services or the coordinator/director of special education should be able to supply you with a student's identification number, gender, racial/ethnic code, school, grade, intelligence range, dates of referral, evaluation and classification, reasons for the referral, and reasons that a student is no longer in the program. However, do not be surprised if this information is not readily available. In one audit, I was not able to get this information readily from a district that had its own computer department; however, with time, I received all this information for almost 100% of the students referred, classified, and/or declassified from special education. It was much more difficult to get information regarding the number of biological parents with whom a student resides. Oftentimes, district forms are incomplete, especially sections that ask for the father's name, address, and business telephone number. The student's socioeconomic status can, as a rule of thumb, be determined by whether the student receives free or reduced lunches. The reasons for referrals should be taken from referral forms completed by teachers; however, if the reasons are not available from teacher referral forms, most of the information can be gathered from summary information found in the psychologists' reports. Also, if these data are not automated and/or cannot be downloaded to your database, it will require time to enter all this data. However, this is time well spent if you want to make sound decisions about the management and operation of the special education program.

There are other sources of information that you need to carry out this audit. You want copies of individual educational plan objectives/criterion, curriculum guides for self-contained special education classes, and curriculum guides from mainstream classes. Also, you need copies of job descriptions for administrators of the special education program, teaching assistants, and teacher aides. Remember, there might not be curriculum guides in place or separate curriculum guides for self-contained special education students. Also, there might not be updated job descriptions or any job descriptions. What a wonderful opportunity! This allows you to suggest a curriculum design and to develop job descriptions and evaluation instruments for each position and present these as part of your summative report.

Your state education department should be able to supply you with data that allows you to compare the percent of students in your district that are classified with the percent of students in your county and state that are classified by handicapping condition. Your state education department and/or your district should be able to provide you with data about resident students provided special education by other districts and/or by intermediate units. They should be able to provide you with data about the percent of time that students are outside their regular classrooms and the type of segregated settings such as special public day school or home, hospital or other non-school, where students from your district receive service. Finally, your state education department and/or district should be able to supply you with the regulations on special education for your state. Remember, when you present your report and if your report indicates numbers that appear to be disproportionate, task force members, faculty, and members of the board of education will want to compare the data locally and statewide. Also, data from official state education reports permit you to doublecheck the figures from your own district.

In addition to hard data, you will need anecdotal information to flesh out all the data. You need to survey all groups that have a role in the referral, classification, and declassification processes. However, you need to make sure that the people surveyed know that you will guarantee their anonymity and confidentiality. More often than not, you want a group perception on an issue and not an individual perception, so you do not need the names of participants. Also, give the people surveyed at least two weeks to complete the form and have them return the form directly to you or a secretary that you designate.

ILLUSTRATION: METHOD TO DETERMINE NUMBER OF PEOPLE TO SURVEY

The number of people you survey depends upon the size of your special education program. If your district has fewer than 300 classified students, you can survey all classroom teachers, all special education teachers, all principals, all psychologists, all social workers, and all parents. If your school district has over 1000 classified students, you need to sample some groups. The number of teachers to survey is determined by the percent of classified students by grade level. If there are 1000 classified students and 100 of them are third graders, then 10% of the third-grade teachers would be surveyed. If 600 of the 1000 students are classified LD, then 60% of the parents/guardians surveyed would be parents/guardians of LD students.

For example, in one district that had over 2000 classified students, separate surveys were developed for each group in this study based upon the percent of classified students by grade level and classification. Two hundred regular classroom teachers were part of a random stratified survey. Forty-one percent of teachers (82) taught grades K−2, 31% of teachers (62) taught grades 3−6, 10% of teachers (20) taught grades 7−8, 11% of teachers (22) taught grades 9−10, and 7% of teachers (14) taught grades 11−12. All sixteen psychologists, all 137 special education teachers, and all sixteen building principals were surveyed. Five hundred parents were surveyed. This included 257 parents of students classified LD, 104 parents of students classified SI, sixty-one parents of students classified ED, thirty parents of students classified OHI, and forty-eight parents of students with other classifications. All CSE members who were not surveyed as either regular or special education teachers, psychologists, parents, or administrators completed the survey. Remember, people might not complete the survey. We have had return rates from different groups of people that ranged from 14% to 100%. However, the album you create is more complete than what presently exists in your district/school. Your study will present insights into the management and operation of special education that will help your district improve services to children. The true wealth of this study is that it provides information that is specifically yours.

On the following pages are suggested surveys for the different groups that have a stake in the management and operation of the special education program. Along with each survey form is a boilerplate for a database to automate responses. Please feel free to reproduce these surveys or modify them to meet your unique needs.

All the responses from classroom teachers (Chart 2.1) can be codified and entered into a database file that allows you to determine relationships between variables. A boilerplate for the database includes the fields and the width of each field. Remember, there is always one more field than on the survey. You need a field to identify each survey form, a form/teacher identification number. The boilerplate for the responses from classroom teachers includes

Field	Width in Characters
1. Classroom teacher's identification number	3
2. Classroom teacher's gender	2
3. Years of full-time teaching	3
4. Number of credits in special education courses	3
5. Has classroom teacher referred students	2
6. Number of students referred	3
7A. Knowledge of district criteria for placement	2
7B. Who informed classroom teacher of requirements	2
8. Problems that triggered referral	2
9. Prereferral actions by teacher	8
10. Classroom teacher's purpose in referring students	8
11. Role of special education personnel in classroom teacher's decision to refer students	2
12. Role of building administrator in classroom teacher's decision to refer students	2
13. Reason more males than females referred	2
14. Reason why large numbers of referred students come from single-parent households	2
15. Suggestions	2

All the responses from special education teachers (Chart 2.2) can be codified and entered into a database file that allows you to determine relationships between variables. A boilerplate for the database includes the fields and the width of each field. Remember, there is always one more field than on the survey. You need a field to identify each survey form, a form/special education teacher identification number. The boilerplate for the responses from special education teachers includes

Field	Width in Characters
1. Special education teacher's identification number	3
2. Special education teacher's gender	2
3. Years of full-time teaching	3
4. Number of credits in special education courses	3
5A. Whether the district has written criteria for placement of students in special education	2
5B. Criteria for LD	3
5C. Criteria for ED	3
6. Role played in the referral process	3
7. Purpose of classroom teacher's referral	3
8. Reason more males than females referred	3
9. Reason a large number of referred students come from single-parent households	3
10. Reason that your district has a greater percent of students classified SI than the county and state	2
11. Reason the average classified student spent approximately forty-six months in special education	2
12. Reason the average student classified LD spent fifty-one months and ED students thirty-six months in special education	4
13A. Role of building administrator in supervising special education classes	2

CHART 2.1 **Classroom Teachers—Survey.**

GRADE/DEPARTMENT _____

SCHOOL _____

You have been specifically selected for inclusion in a sample of teachers who are asked about the referral, classification, and declassification processes for the (Your District). These processes may be modified based on the feedback that is received from you and the rest of the teachers included in this sample. Your help is crucial in assuring that the modifications result in improvement in these processes. All information you provide is confidential. Please complete and return this form by (Date) to _____. Thank you for your help.

Please complete the following demographic information.

1. Female ____   Male ____

2. Years of full-time teaching in (Your School District) _____

3. Number of credits you have in special education courses _____

4. Have you referred students for evaluation for special education? Yes ____   No ____   (If you have not referred students, please stop here and return this form.)

5. Estimate the number of students you referred for special education this last academic year (1995–1996) _____

6. Do you know the legal and/or district criteria for student placement in special education? Yes ____   No ____
If you answered Yes, who informed you of the requirements? _____
_____
_____

7. What are the major difficulties/problems students have that trigger your referral for an evaluation for special education?
_____
_____
_____

8. What actions do you take before students (prereferral) are referred for evaluation for special education?
_____
_____
_____

9. What is your purpose in referring students for evaluation for special education?
_____
_____
_____

10. What role, if any, have special education (psychologists, speech therapists, special education teachers) personnel played in your decision to refer students for evaluation?
_____
_____
_____

11. What role, if any, has your building administrator played in your referrals of students for special education?
_____
_____
_____

12. There are more males (65%) than females (35%) referred for special education. Why do you think this is so?
_____
_____
_____

13. Approximately 44% of the students referred for special education are from homes headed by a single parent. Why do you think this is so?
_____
_____
_____

14. Do you have any suggestions as to how the district might continue the quality of education for students and yet reduce the number of students referred for special education?
_____
_____
_____

CHART 2.2 **Special Education Teachers—Survey.**

GRADE/RESOURCE ROOM _____

SCHOOL _____

You have been specifically selected for inclusion in a sample of special education teachers who are asked about the referral, classification, and declassification processes for the (Your District). These processes may be modified based on the feedback that is received from you and the rest of the special education teachers included in this sample. Your help is crucial in assuring that the modifications result in improvement in these processes. All information you provide is confidential. Please complete and return this form by (Date) to _____. Thank you for your help.

Please complete the following demographic information.

1. Female ____   Male ____

2. Years of full-time teaching in the Special Education Department in the (Your School District) _____

3. Number of credits you have in special education courses _____

4. Does the district have written criteria for student placement in special education? Yes ____   No ____
If you answered Yes, what is the criteria for student classification as:

A. LD _____
_____
_____

B. ED _____
_____
_____

5. What role, if any, do you have in the referral process in your building?
_____
_____
_____

6. What do you think classroom teachers hope to gain for a student by referring the student for an evaluation for special education?
_____
_____
_____

7. There are more males (65%) than females (35%) referred for special education. Why do you think this is so?
_____
_____
_____

8. Approximately 44% of the students referred for special education are from homes headed by a single parent. Why do you think this is so?
_____
_____
_____

9. The percent of students in (Your District) that are classified SI is greater than the percentage in the county and the state. Why do you think this is so?
_____
_____
_____

10. The average classified student spent approximately forty-six months in special education. Why do you think this is so?
_____
_____
_____

11. The average student classified as LD spent fifty-one months in special education, while the average ED student spent thirty-six months in special education. Why do you think this is so?
_____
_____
_____

12. What role, if any, does your building administrator and director of special education play in supervising your classes? Please discuss each position separately.

(continued)

CHART 2.2 (continued).

A. Building administrator _____

_____

_____

B. Director of special education _____

_____

_____

13. What criteria are used to mainstream students?

_____

_____

_____

14. Does the district have written criteria for the declassification of students from special education? Yes ____No ____
If you answered Yes, what is the district criteria for declassification of students from special education?

_____

_____

_____

15. How do you think your students would fare in a regular class?

_____

_____

_____

16. Describe the tasks of your teaching assistant.

_____

_____

_____

17. In terms of your direct experience, what has been the effect of increasing student teacher ratio from 12:1 to 15:1?

_____

_____

_____

18A. What standards/criteria would you use to evaluate the success of the special education program?

_____

_____

_____

B. What special education programs are successful?

_____

_____

_____

C. What special education programs are not successful?

_____

_____

_____

19. Do you have any suggestions as to how the district might improve the management and operation of the special education program?

_____

_____

_____

Field	Width in Characters
13B. Role of director of special education in supervising special education classes	2
14. Criteria to mainstream students	8
15A. Whether the district has criteria to declassify students	2
15B. What the criteria are to declassify students	8
16. Student's performance in a regular class	2
17. Tasks of a teaching assistant	8
18. Effect of increasing class size to 15:1	8
19A. Standards to evaluate special education program	4
19B. Special education programs that are successful	8
19C. Special education programs that are not successful	8
20. Suggestions	8

All the responses from psychologists (Chart 2.3) can be codified and entered into a database file that allows you to determine relationships between variables. A boilerplate for the database includes the fields and the width of each field. Remember, there is always one more field than on the survey. You need a field to identify each survey form, a psychologist identification number. The boilerplate for the responses from psychologists includes

Field	Width in Characters
1. Psychologist's identification number	3
2. Psychologist's gender	2
3. Years as a full-time psychologist	3
4. Number of credits in special education courses	3
5. Whether the district has written criteria for placement of students in special education	2
5A. Criteria for LD	3
5B. Criteria for ED	3
5C. Criteria for SI	3
5D. Criteria for OHI	3
6. Role played in the referral process	3
7. Purpose of classroom teacher's referral	3

Field	Width in Characters
8. Reason more males than females referred	3
9. Reason a large number of referred students come from single-parent households	3
10. Reason that your district has a greater percent of students classified SI than the county and state	2
11A. Relevancy of classroom teacher statements	2
11B. Relevancy of assessment data	2
12. Reason for classification of high school students	2
13. Reason that students are classified LD longer than ED	2
14. Difference between LD and low-achieving students	8
15A. Assessment devices used by name	20
15B. Technical adequacy of each assessment device	8
16A. Whether the district has criteria to declassify students	2
16B. What the criteria are to declassify students	8
17A. Role of the CSE as chairperson	8
17B. Role when not chairperson compared to other members	8
18. CSE as a gatekeeper	2
19. Suggestions	8

All the responses from CSE members (Chart 2.4) can be codified and entered into a database file that allows you to determine relationships between variables. A boilerplate for the database includes the fields and the width of each field. Remember, there is always one more field than on the survey. You need a field to identify each survey form, a CSE member identification number. The boilerplate for the responses from CSE members includes

Field	Width in Characters
1. CSE member's identification number	3
2. CSE member's gender	2
3. Years as a CSE member	3
4. Number of credits in special education courses	3
5A. Whether the district has written criteria for placement of students in special education	2

CHART 2.3 Psychologists—Survey.

SCHOOL _____

You have been specifically selected for inclusion in a sample of psychologists who are asked about the referral, classification, and declassification processes for the (Your District). These processes may be modified based on the feedback that is received from you and the rest of the psychologists included in this sample. Your help is crucial in assuring that the modifications result in improvement in these processes. All information you provide is confidential. Please complete and return this form by (Date) to _____. Thank you for your help.

Please complete the following demographic information.

1. Female ____ Male ____

2. Years as a full-time psychologist in the (Your School District) _____

3. Number of credits you have in special education courses _____

4. Does the district have written criteria for student placement in special education? Yes ____ No ____
If you answered Yes, what is the district criteria for student classification as LD, ED, SI, and OHI? If you answered No, what is your criteria for student classification as LD and ED?

A. LD_____
_____

B. ED_____
_____

C. SI_____
_____

D. OHI_____
_____

5. What role, if any, do you have in the referral process in your building? in other buildings?
_____
_____
_____

6. What do you think classroom teachers hope to gain for a student by referring the student for an evaluation for special education?
_____
_____
_____

7. There are more males (65%) than females (35%) referred for special education. Why do you think this is so?
_____
_____
_____

8. Approximately 44% of the students referred for special education are from homes headed by a single parent. Why do you think this is so?
_____
_____
_____

9. The percent of students in (Your District) that are classified SI is greater than the percentage in the county and the state. Why do you think this is so?
_____
_____
_____

10. How relevant are classroom teacher statements and assessment data to decision making regarding the classification of students? Please discuss each item separately.
A. Classroom teacher statements _____
_____
_____

B. Assessment data _____
_____
_____

CHART 2.3 **(continued).**

11. Sixty-eight district high school students were classified in the academic year 1993–1994. Some of these were students that transferred to (Your District) from other districts. However, some were in your district. Why do you think students so advanced in age would be classified for the first time? On what basis do you think they were classified?

_____
_____
_____

12. The average student classified as LD was classified for a longer period of time than a student classified ED. Why do you think this is so?

_____
_____
_____

13. What is the difference between low achieving students and students labeled learning disabled?

_____
_____
_____

14A. What assessment devices do you use (name the specific instruments)?

_____
_____
_____

B. How technically adequate are each of these assessment devices?

_____
_____
_____

15. Does the district have written criteria for the declassification of students from special education? Yes _____ No _____
If you answered Yes, what are the district criteria for declassification of students from special education?

_____
_____
_____

16A. What is your role on the CSE when you serve as chairperson?

_____
_____
_____

B. What is your unique role on the CSE, when you are not chairperson, compared to other members of the CSE?

_____
_____
_____

17. How well do you think the CSE serves as an effective gatekeeper for males, minorities, and students from low socioeconomic backgrounds?

_____
_____
_____

18. Do you have any suggestions regarding how the district might improve the management and operation of the special education program?

_____
_____
_____

CHART 2.4 **CSE Members—Survey.**

You have been specifically selected for inclusion in a sample of CSE members who are asked about the referral, classification and declassification processes for the (Your District). These processes may be modified based on the feedback that is received from you and the rest of the CSE members included in this sample. Your help is crucial in assuring that the modifications result in improvement in these processes. All information you provide is confidential. Please complete and return this form by (Date) to _____. Thank you for your help.

Please complete the following demographic information.

1. Female ____ Male ____

2. Years as a CSE member in the (Your School District)_____

3. Number of credits you have in special education courses _____

4. Does the district have written criteria for student placement in special education? Yes ___ No ____
If you answered Yes, what is the criteria for student classification as:
A. LD _____
_____

B. ED _____
_____

5. What do you think classroom teachers hope to gain for a student by referring the student for an evaluation for special education?
_____
_____
_____

6. There are more males (65%) than females (35%) referred for special education. Why do you think this is so?
_____
_____
_____

7. Approximately 44% of the students referred for special education are from homes headed by a single parent. Why do you think this is so?
_____
_____
_____

8. The percent of students in (Your District) that are classified SI is greater than the percentage in the county and the state. Why do you think this is so?
_____
_____
_____

9. How often do you attend CSE meetings? _____
10. How does the CSE decide on student placement (process)?
_____
_____
_____

11. Who attends the CSE meetings and how frequently?
_____
_____
_____

12. What role does the psychologist play in the classification process? What role do other members play?
_____
_____
_____

13. What pressure, if any, is felt by CSE members?
_____
_____
_____

CHART 2.4 (continued).

14. What role does the director of special education and the assistant superintendent for pupil personnel services play in CSE meetings?

_____
_____
_____

15. What criteria is used to mainstream students?

_____
_____
_____

16. Does the district have written criteria for the declassification of students from special education? Yes ____ No ___
If you answered Yes, what is the district criteria for declassification of students from special education?

_____
_____
_____

17. Do you have any suggestions as to how the district might improve the management and operation of the special education program?

_____
_____
_____

Field	Width in Characters
5B. Criteria for LD	3
5C. Critera for ED	3
6. Purpose of classroom teacher's referral	3
7. Reason more males than females referred	3
8. Reason a large number of referred students come from single-parent homes	3
9. Reason that your district has a greater percent of students classified SI than the county and state	2
10. Attendance at CSE meetings	2
11. Decision-making process for classification	8
12. Attendance of CSE members	8
13. Role of psychologist in the classification process	4
14. Pressure experienced	2
15A. Role of the director of special education at CSE meetings	2
15B. Role of the assistant superintendent for pupil personnel services at CSE meetings	2
16. Criteria used to mainstream students	8
17A. Whether the district has criteria to declassify students	2

Field	Width in Characters
17B. What the criteria are to declassify students	8
18. Suggestions	4

All the responses from principals (Chart 2.5) can be codified and entered into a database file that allows you to determine relationships between variables. A boilerplate for the database includes the fields and the width of each field. Remember, there is always one more field than on the survey. You need a field to identify each survey form, a principal identification number. The boilerplate for the responses from principals includes

Field	Width in Characters
1. CSE member's identification number	3
2. CSE member's gender	2
3. Years as a CSE member	3
4. Number of credits in special education courses	3
5. Whether the district has written criteria for placement of students in special education	2
5A. Criteria for LD	3
5B. Criteria for ED	3
6. Role in the prereferral process	4
7. Role in the referral process	4
8. Purpose of classroom teacher's referral	3

CHART 2.5 Principals—Survey.

SCHOOL (CIRCLE ONE) ELEMENTARY MIDDLE SCHOOL HIGH SCHOOL

You have been specifically selected for inclusion in a sample of principals who are asked about the referral, classification, and declassification processes for the (Your District). These processes may be modified based on the feedback that is received from you and the rest of the special education personnel included in this sample. Your help is crucial in assuring that the modifications result in improvement in these processes. All information you provide is confidential. Please complete and return this form by (Date) and return to _____. Thank you for your help.

Please complete the following demographic information.

1. Female _____ Male _____

2. Years as an administrator in the (Your School District) _____

3. Number of credits you have in special education courses _____

4. Does the district have written criteria for student placement in special education? Yes _____ No _____
If you answered Yes, what is the criteria for student classification as:
A. LD _____
_____
_____

B. ED _____
_____
_____

5. What role, if any, do you have in the prereferral process?
_____
_____
_____

6. What role, if any, do you have in the referral process?
_____
_____
_____

7. What do you think classroom teachers hope to gain for a student by referring the student for an evaluation for special education?
_____
_____
_____

8. There are more males (65%) than females (35%) referred for special education. Why do you think this is so?
_____
_____
_____

9. Approximately 44% of the students referred for special education are from homes headed by a single parent. Why do you think this is so?
_____
_____
_____

10. The percent of students in (Your District) that are classified SI is greater than the percentage in the county and the state. Why do you think this is so?
_____
_____
_____

11. How often do you attend CSE meetings?
_____
_____
_____

12. How relevant is assessment data to the decision-making process?
_____
_____
_____

CHART 2.5 (continued).

13. How relevant is a teacher's statement to the decision-making process?

_____

_____

_____

14. What role does the psychologist play in the classification process in comparison to other members of the CSE?

_____

_____

_____

15. The average classified student spent approximately forty-six months in special education. Why do you think this is so?

_____

_____

_____

16. The average student classified as LD spent fifty-one months in special education while the average ED student spent thirty-six months in special education. Why do you think this is so?

_____

_____

_____

17. What role, if any, do you, the assistant superintendent for pupil personnel services, and the director of special education play in supervising your special education classes? How many times is a class observed formally and informally? Please discuss each position separately.
A. Building administrator

_____

_____

_____

B. Assistant superintendent for pupil personnel services

_____

_____

_____

C. Director of special education

_____

_____

_____

18. What is your role in supervising, monitoring, and evaluating special education curriculum?

_____

_____

19. What criteria is used to mainstream students?

_____

_____

20. Does the district have written criteria for the declassification of students from special education? Yes _____ No _____
If you answered Yes, what is the district criteria for declassification of students from special education?

_____

_____

21. In terms of your direct experience what has been the effect of increasing student teacher ratio from 12:1 to 15:1?

_____

_____

22A. How are teaching assistants used in 15:1 classes?

_____

_____

(continued)

CHART 2.5 (continued).

B. What thoughts do you have regarding the use of teaching assistants in 15:1 classes?

_____

_____

_____

23. Do you have any suggestions as to how the district might improve the management and operation of the special education program?

_____

_____

_____

Field	Width in Characters
9. Reason more males than females referred	3
10. Reason a large number of referred students come from single-parent households	3
11. Reason that your district has a greater percent of students classified SI than the county and state	2
12. Attendance at CSE meetings	2
13. Relevancy of assessment data to decision-making process	2
14. Relevancy of teacher's statements to decision-making process	2
15. Role of psychologist in classification process	2
16. Reason the average classified student spent approximately forty-six months in special education	2
17. Reason the average student classified LD spent fifty-one months and ED students thirty-six months in special education	4
18A. Role of building administrator in supervising special education classes	2
18B. Role of assistant superintendent for pupil personnel services in supervising special education classes	2
18C. Role of director of special education in supervising special education classes	2
19. Role in supervising, monitoring, and evaluating special education curriculum	2
20. Criteria to mainstream students	8
21A. Whether the district has criteria to declassify students	2
21B. What the criteria are to declassify students	8
22. Effect of increasing class size to 15:1	8
23A. Tasks of a teaching assistant in 15:1 classes	8
23B. Thoughts about use of teaching assistants in 15:1 classes	8
24. Suggestions	8

Parents, as consumers or clients (Chart 2.6), need to be surveyed because they can tell you whether they are satisfied with their treatment and the treatment of their children by administrative, regular classroom, and special education personnel; have had their children dealt with in a timely fashion; perceive the program as suitable for their children; and have thoughts about the strengths and weaknesses of the special education program. In order to get this information, you have to mail the survey to selected parents with a stamped addressed return envelope.

All the responses from parents can be codified and entered into a database file that allows you to determine relationships between variables. A boilerplate for the database includes the fields and the width of each field. Remember, there is always one more field than on the survey. You need a field to identify each survey form, a parent identification number. The boilerplate for the responses from parents includes

Field	Width in Characters
1. Parent's identification number	3
2A. Number of children in special education	2
2B. Ages of children	10
2C. Classification of each child	10

CHART 2.6 **Parents—Survey.**

You have been specifically selected for inclusion in a sample of parents who are asked about the referral, classification, and declassification processes for the (Your District). These processes may be modified based on the feedback that is received from you and the rest of the parents included in this sample. Your help is crucial in assuring that the modifications result in improvement in these processes. All information you provide is confidential. Please return your completed survey by (Date). Thank you for your help.

1. How many children do you have in special education programs? _____

Ages/Grades	Years in Program	Classification
_____	_____	_____
_____	_____	_____
_____	_____	_____
_____	_____	_____

2. What are the pluses and minuses of the type of program (self-contained class, resource, mainstreamed, or regular education program) that your child is in from the point of view of your child?

_____
_____
_____

3. How would you describe your dealings with the Committee on Special Education (CSE)?

_____
_____
_____

4A. Why was your child recommended for special education?

_____
_____
_____

B. What steps, if any, were taken by the teacher in the mainstream class to remediate the difficulties that your child had in school?

_____
_____
_____

C. Who informed you of the criteria for student placement in special education?

_____
_____
_____

5. How would you describe your dealings with the special education department?

_____
_____
_____

6. Describe the progress made by your child since she/he has been in the special education program.

_____
_____
_____

7A. Has your child been mainstreamed for any part of the school day? _____
B. Describe your child's experience when he/she was mainstreamed.

_____
_____
_____

8. What do you view as the strengths of the special education program for your child?

_____
_____
_____

(continued)

CHART 2.6 (continued).

9. What concerns do you have about the special education program as it relates to your child?

_____
_____
_____

10. What thoughts do you have about the subjects that your child studies?

_____
_____
_____

11A. How has your child been treated by other children, in school and on the bus?

_____
_____
_____

B. How has your child been treated by both special education and mainstream teachers?

_____
_____
_____

C. How has your child been treated by administrators?

_____
_____
_____

12. Overall, how would you rate the special education program?

_____
_____
_____

13. Do you have any suggestions regarding how the program could be altered to better meet the needs of your child?

_____
_____
_____

14. Do you have any suggestions regarding how the district might improve the management and operation of the special education program?

_____
_____
_____

Field	Width in Characters
3A. Pluses of program	10
3B. Minuses of program	10
4. Dealings with committee on special education	3
5A. Reason child referred	8
5B. Steps to remediate difficulties	8
5C. Person who informed you of criteria for placement	2
6. Dealings with special education department	3
7. Progress made by child	3
8A. Whether child has been mainsteamed	2
8B. Describe experience for child	2
9. Strengths of the special education program	8
10. Concerns about the special education program	8
11. Thoughts about subjects studied	8
12A. Treatment by other children in school or on bus	2
12B. Treatment by special education and mainstream teachers	2
12C. Treatment by administrators	2
13. Overall rating of special education program	2
14. Suggestions to alter program for your child	2
15. Suggestions to improve management and operation of the special education program	2

You now have in place your survey forms and database files necessary to implement your audit of the management and operation of special education. You now need to establish your special education task force in order to legitimize the process and verify your findings, conclusions, and recommendations.

SPECIAL EDUCATION TASK FORCE

In this day and age, it is expected that the school community needs to have systematic input into decisions that they are to implement and/or live with. No one, least of all an experienced school administrator, doubts that this means a bumpy ride. Decision making takes longer. There are irrelevant observations. People grandstand. There are private and not so private agendas. And rather than a majority opinion, there is a consensus. Someone once said that a meaningful faculty meeting is an oxymoron much like military intelligence, congressional ethics, and jumbo shrimp. Another remarked that a camel is a horse created by a school committee. As tedious and demanding as committees are, they are necessary if one wants the members of the school community to grow and if one wants to make sure that the community has a clear understanding of all the facts and issues related to the management and operation of special education. It is the best way to ensure that members of the Special Education Parent Teacher Association (SEPTA) will not be manipulated by those who wish to stonewall any modifications in the management and operation of the special education program.

You need to set up a special education task force (SETF) of school personnel and parents to help you with this audit. You need to give thought to the composition of the SETF, the number of people on the SETF, and the frequency of meetings. The purpose of this involvement is to (1) ensure members of the school community that the analysis is objective; (2) review questionnaires and survey documents to ensure that the information retrieved is usable; (3) be sensitive to the concerns of administrators, teachers, parents, and students; (4) anticipate and resolve possible problems related to the retrieval of data; and (5) resolve questions about preliminary report findings.

In addition to the assistant superintendent for pupil personnel services and/or the director for special education, the SETF should be made up of principals, classroom teachers, special education teachers, psychologists, guidance counselors, speech therapists, social workers, parents, and members of the board of education. Give a great deal of care to the composition of the SETF. When people are not worried that their findings will result in a reduction of positions and/or a reflection on their professional competency, but truly

want to improve the processes, the SETF is a sound example of the wealth of information and different perspectives that people bring to an issue. Otherwise it becomes a struggle for reality testing. Nevertheless, it is necessary. At its best, it is an educational process for all participants. A white female assistant superintendent for pupil personnel put together a team of people that brought all kinds of insights to bear upon data that pointed out the disproportionate representation of minority and male students referred for evaluation for placement in special education and eventually classified. The SETF members did not try to rationalize these data by pointing out that this was a national phenomenon but rather suggested ways to get at the root causes of this in their district.

At its worst, the findings are either denied, placed in national perspective and dismissed, denied a national perspective and dismissed, and/or explained away. In one instance, an SETF argued vehemently over the word *disproportionate*. The word was used to note that 65% of referred students were males. The SETF members objected to using *disproportionate* to describe the fact that minority students made up 4% of the district's student population, but 9% of the students classified as emotionally handicapped. One SETF member said that it did not cause him a problem. Others pointed out that this was a national trend. There were objections to studies such as those by Dr. Figueroa, which pointed out the lack of integrity of school psychologists nationally, from being included in a literature review in a summative report because the SETF feared it might reflect on the district's psychologists.

When it was pointed out that there were not any formal locally written criteria in place for classification and declassification, it was dismissed on the basis that competent people were making decisions. When it was noted that there were not any formal, local curriculum guides in place for social studies for students in self-contained classes, it was argued first that the curriculum guides were the same as those used in the mainstream remedial classes, and when there were questions regarding the appropriateness of the breadth and depth of the curriculum for self-contained students, the cry went up that the mainstream program lacked curriculum guides. Although there was a concerted effort by some members of the SETF to deny any problems with the management and operation of the special education program, slowly but surely, issues were put on the table and problems acknowledged. Notwithstanding the tediousness of the process, this was a learning experience for most members of the SETF, especially for members of the board of education. If the adage is that, without pain, there is no growth, then these people grew to be at least ten feet tall. Ultimately, the SETF understood that (1) the way to fix the special education program is to improve the mainstream program and (2) programs can work effectively and efficiently when students are placed properly, curriculum is in place, principals take ownership of programs in their buildings, services are evaluated, and turf wars are eliminated.

The size of the SETF has varied from eight to seventeen members. Make sure that there is a balance in members. Do not overload the committee with any one group of people. And please do not be surprised if people turn out to behave differently than you expected. All you want from these members is their insights and for them to keep an open mind about the findings from the audit. And that is a great deal. You expect people to have different levels of knowledge about the management and operation of special education. Remember all these people will grow.

This audit will take you approximately twenty hours of research and writing time to complete, excluding meetings, for an elementary school of 500 regular students; forty hours for a high school of 1500 regular students; sixty hours for a district of 3000 students; and 150 hours for a district of 15,000 students. Time varies based upon the type and amount of information that is already automated by the district. SETF meetings need to be held twice a month. The length of time you allow for each meeting is related to the size of your special education population, but meetings should not exceed two hours each. When possible materials should be given to members of the SETF before meetings. However, that is not possible at all times if you want to complete the audit in less than six months. Therefore, be prepared to explain your findings to the group. Use charts and overheads whenever possible. Write out any questions you have that you want the group to discuss and put these questions on an overhead. When you have finished your first draft of your audit report, give it to the group to read. Remind them that the information in the report is sensitive and not to be shared with anyone but members of the SETF until it is presented to the superintendent or board of education. Allow them a week to read the report and make corrections or suggestions. Listen to their comments carefully. Normally, there are merely cosmetic changes suggested, and if you update your draft after each meeting these changes can be accommodated easily. However, substantive changes should only be made if there is supportive material to warrant the change. If you do your job well, there should not be any surprises and few changes in the draft.

You may now begin your audit. You will find it a fascinating undertaking, one that will give you tremendous insights into the actual management and operation of the program. Good luck.

3

Quick Overview of Your Special Education Program

AIM

THE purpose of this chapter is to have you develop an overview of your special education program, compare the size of your program with those of other districts in your county and state, and determine the human and financial resources you use to deliver the special education program as presently constituted. All this information is readily available from either state and/or district reports, requires minimal time on your part to analyze, and is essential to present to members of your SETF to place your special education program in perspective. There is a wealth of information about the management and operation of the special education program that is at your fingertips once your database is updated, information from your district and state education department is secured, and you have analyzed completed survey forms. This chapter provides you with boilerplates to use in writing your summative report and illustrations of findings from audits to clarify specific points.

INTRODUCTION

Before you present the results of your audit, you need to provide an overview of the size and cost of the special education program as a method to place your program in perspective and to highlight some reasons to warrant this audit. This involves an analysis of five or six one-page reports from your state education department and/or your district/school and a summary of expenditures that are normally forwarded to the state education department by your business office. This material can be presented to the SETF at the first meeting. Members of the SETF want to know

- How does the percent of students in your program compare with neighboring schools of similar size and populations and the rest of the state?

- How many special education teachers are employed by the district?
- How much does the special education program cost?

Data for this portion of the audit is readily available from the state education department and/or your own district. These data point out trends about your district in comparison to those in your county and state. However, you need to keep in mind that information from state reports might reflect the number of classified and enrolled students as of October or December of the year, rather than for June. If you want to use data that reflect findings for the entire academic year (June), you will not be able to make a valid comparison with other districts in your county and state.

ILLUSTRATION: PERCENT OF CLASSIFIED STUDENTS

Chart 3.1 indicates that District A has a greater percent of students classified speech impaired than does the county or state; however, District A has a smaller percent of students classified learning disabled and emotionally handicapped than the county and state. Also, a smaller percent of students from District A are serviced outside the district. Remember you have to put percentage points in perspective. If District A had 2077 classified students out of a total population of 14,457 students, 1% of students would equal 145 students $(14,457 \times .01)$. Therefore, for District A to have the same percent (11.8%) of students as the state average would mean that the district needed to have 348 fewer students in the program (145×2.4). In other words, the number of classified students would be reduced from 2077 to 1729. If there were 453 students in District A classified speech impaired and if District A wanted to have the same percent (13.2%) of students classified speech impaired as in the state, the district would have to have 179 fewer students or $453 - 179 = 274$ students

CHART 3.1 Comparison of District A, County, and State in Percent.

	Your District	County	State
Overall	14.2	13.7	11.8
SI	21.8	15.8	13.2
LD	52.6	58.4	59.7
ED	11.4	11.6	12.2
Services provided outside the district	5.8	10.7	7.6

in the special education program ($13.2/21.8 \times x/453$). In other words, a change of one percentage point for speech impaired involves 21 students.

BOILERPLATE: PERCENT OF CLASSIFIED STUDENTS

Use Chart 3.1 or a bar graph to present your data to the SETF. These are easy to understand and require minimal time on your part to put together. Once you have discussed these data with the SETF, write your draft introduction for a summative report. You can use Chart 3.1 or bar graphs in your written summative report, or you can just put the information in a paragraph or you can use a combination of both graphics and narrative. The boilerplate for the introduction allows you to insert these data. The boilerplate reads:

The percent of students classified in the district (14.2%), for the academic year, exceeded the state's average of 11.8% and the county's average of 13.7%. There were 2077 classified students and 12,470 nonclassified students enrolled in the district, or a total of 14,547 students. The percent of special education students classified speech impaired in the district (21.8%) exceeded the state's (13.2%) and the county's averages (15.8%). The percent of special education students classified learning disabled (52.6%) was less than the state's (59.7%) and the county's averages (58.4%). The percent of students classified emotionally disturbed (11.4%) that received regular classroom instruction and related services was less than the state's (12.2%) and the county's (11.6%). Furthermore, the percent (5.8%) of the district's students that received services from another school district and/or an intermediate unit was less than the state (7.6%) and county (10.7%).

For a district with 440 students, this introduction reads:

The percent of students classified in your district (13.8), for the academic year, exceeded the state's

average of 10.8%, and county's average of 12.3%. There were 440 classified students and 2740 non-classified students enrolled in your district, or a total of 3180 students. The percent of special education students classified as ED, MH, and MR was lower than the county's average. However, the percent of special education students classified LD was 64.7% compared to the county's average of 59.5%. The percent of special education students classified SI was 15.9% compared to the county's average of 14%.

At the very least, this introduction provides your district with an overview that places your special education program in perspective with other districts in your county and state. Also, it indicates the number of students that would either not receive or receive services to meet the county and state averages. The first question that one has to grapple with when your district exceeds county and state averages is why this situation exists in your district. Is there a better screening procedure? Are parents pushing for classification? Or are there other reasons? If so, what are those reasons?

Other data from the state education department sheds light on the human and financial resources needed to support the special education program. This information is important to you as you plan to use local, state, and federal funds to deliver the best possible program for your students. State education departments generate reports that point out the number of people employed and/or full-time equivalent (FTE) special education teachers to service those students who attended school in the district. Because these data are gathered from individual teachers and/or district personnel, there are questions raised about the accuracy of details, but not totals. However, the overall number of teachers shows the human resources needed for the special education program. Remember, the program is not monolithic. A large program, one that services 2077 students had 153 FTEs while a program that services 440 students had thirty-seven special education teachers. There is obviously an economy of scale. Namely, the larger program services 4.7 times as many students as the smaller program but requires 4.1 times as many teachers.

ILLUSTRATION: NUMBER OF SPECIAL EDUCATION TEACHERS

The school community needs to be aware that some special education teachers are used solely for students with specific handicapping conditions, that is, mentally retarded, elementary resource room; hard of hearing, special class—JHS; speech impaired, special class—elementary; or learning disabled, special class—HS. Other special education teachers work with students in their class who have different handicapping conditions. An illustration of the number of employees needed to service students in different size programs can be gathered from the two districts cited. The larger district had forty-one special education teachers and the smaller program had eighteen special education teachers to service solely learning disabled students.

Large District

Course Name	Number of Teachers (FTEs)
LD, Resource room—elementary	19.047
LD, Resource room—JHS	5.649
LD, Resource room—HS	1.600
LD, Special class—elementary	14.000
LD, Special class—HS	1.400

Small District

Course Name	Number of Teachers (FTEs)
LD, Preschool resource room or special class	2.0
LD, Elementary resource room	1.2
LD, Jr. high resource room	0.8
LD, High school resource room	3.0
LD, Elementary special class	7.0
LD, Jr. high special class	3.0
LD, High school special class	1.2

Also, you need to know the number and percent of students that spend their time in special education. The New York State Education Department issues a report entitled "Number of Students with Disabilities Provided Special Education in Regular School Based Programs," which indicates the percent of time classified students spend outside regular classrooms. It spells out the percent of students that spend no more than 20% of their time outside the regular classroom, 21%—60% of their time outside the regular classroom, and more than 60% of their time outside the regular classroom. In addition, state education departments report on the percent of students in segregated settings,

including special public day school, special private day school, and private residential facilities. Members of the school board of education, members of the SETF, and school personnel want to know whether the data for your district/school is similar to that of other districts/schools in your county and state. If there is a difference, they would value your thoughts on the subject and would welcome an opportunity to share their thoughts with you. Listen carefully to their opinions and determine if there are means to verify their thoughts. All this information needs to be analyzed and evaluated before you write your introduction to your summative report.

Finally, you need to lay out the district's expenditures for special education, including public and private placement. These are million dollar expenditures once you have sixty self-contained special education students in schools with high salary costs and perhaps 100 self-contained special education students in districts with low salary costs. You need to determine the percent of expenditures spent on special education and the percent of students that were serviced. However, you need to be careful not to include educationally related support services (ERSS) funds and to be consistent regarding transportation costs. A high-salary district with 2077 students spent $22 million on special education. The same district received revenues from state aid totaling $11,471,417, excluding any transportation aid. The district with 440 students had expenditures of $3.1 million for special education, including public and private placement. The total amount of aid from the state was $1,628,192. (These sums do not include transportation monies or operating aid or supplemental support aid.) Remember, expenditures are not clean-cut. In one study where the pupil personnel service staff in a high school district worked twenty-six hours a week, they were asked to log their time for twenty to twenty-seven weeks. They indicated the time they spent on the application process, annual reviews, triennial reviews, new referrals, and miscellaneous activities. However, as a group, they could not account for 20% of their work time. The most effective way to present special education expenditures is by function areas:

(1) Administrative/secretarial costs (2016 function area)
(2) Cost of self-contained special education classes (2250 function area)
(3) Committee of special education/preschool education (2251/52 function areas)
(4) Resource room (2255 function area)
(5) Psychologists, social workers/speech therapists (2820/22/25 function areas)

(6) Transportation (5540 – 81 function areas)
(7) Benefits (9000 function areas)
(8) Interfund transfers-pro-rata (9902 function area)
(9) Total budget
(10) Percent of budget

SUMMARY

Remember, the purpose of this chapter is to help you to present an overview of your special education program as a means to focus attention on the management and operation of special education. The broad picture raises questions about reasons for the greater percent of students in your district that are classified SI, LD, or ED.

- Are there issues about the referral process that need to be addressed?
- What criteria and standards are used to determine whether a student needs to be referred for evaluation for placement in special education?
- Why do classroom teachers refer students for evaluation for placement in special education?
- What are the characteristics of students who are referred for evaluation for placement in special education?

Questions are raised regarding the educational outcomes of the program. These questions inevitably lead to other questions about the special education curriculum and student outcomes:

- Are there curriculum guides in place for students in self-contained classes?
- What differences exist in terms of the depth, breadth, and pacing between the special education curriculum and the mainstream program?
- What criteria are used to mainstream students?

Finally, there are questions raised about the declassification process:

- How many students are declassified?
- How does one get declassified?
- What are the characteristics of students who are declassified?

And each of these questions are apt to trigger other questions about the management and operation of the special education program. The following chapters show you how the process unfolds and presents you with practical and usable information to improve the management and operation of the special education program.

4

The First Steps in an Audit of the Referral Process

AIM

THIS chapter explains three types of information you need to gather, methods used to get the information, and ways to present your findings about the referral process as part of the management and operation audit of special education. First, this chapter identifies hard data needed to put student referrals in perspective, that is, data used to develop a profile of teachers who refer students for evaluation for placement in special education and the numbers of students referred for placement in special education for the previous academic year ending June 30th. Second, this chapter explains issues related to classification criteria, supplies a checklist of reasons for referrals by classroom teachers, specifies steps taken by classroom teachers to remediate problems faced by students and reproduces comments by classroom teachers to clarify their reasons for referrals. Third, this chapter shows you how to determine the role played by special education personnel and principals in the referral process in order to evaluate whether they have undue influence on decisions by classroom teachers to refer students for evaluation for placement in special education. Fourth, this chapter walks you through a process that allows you to conclude whether referrals by classroom teachers were tainted by the gender, family status, and/or racial/ethnic background of students. There are many illustrations taken from audits to highlight issues raised in this chapter and to be used by you as a boilerplate to write your summative report. Anecdotal information gathered from classroom teachers, special education teachers, principals, psychologists, and CSE members are used to form a checklist that can be used by you to monitor your referral process. If you follow the steps spelled out in this chapter, you will be able to determine whether the referral process in your district/school is sound or flawed. If the process is jaded, you will be able to identify the steps to take to ensure the equity, objectivity, and effectiveness of this aspect of the manage-

ment and operation of special education. What is more, you will be able to differentiate segments and target actions to specific components of the referral process. As a result, you will be able to reduce the number of students referred for evaluations for placements in special education programs.

PROFILE OF CLASSROOM TEACHERS WHO REFER STUDENTS FOR EVALUATION FOR SPECIAL EDUCATION

To create a well-managed and operated special education program, you first need to ensure the integrity of the referral process. Without this, any attempt to strengthen the management and operation of special education will be as futile as rearranging the deck chairs on the Titanic. In order to guarantee the equity, objectivity, and efficiency of the referral process, you need to analyze data and anecdotal comments by classroom teachers, special education teachers, principals, psychologists, and CSE members.

Your entire faculty, support personnel, and parents of special education students are a rich source of information about the management and operation of your special education program, and they need to be debriefed by you. All anecdotal information and some hard data can only be obtained if these people voluntarily share their thoughts and information with you. And they will cooperate with you if they believe that their anonymity and confidentiality will be respected and if they believe that their comments will be weighed carefully. This is especially true of classroom teachers who have referred students for evaluation for placement in special education. They are the only people who can tell you (1) the intervention strategies they tried before they referred students for evaluation for placement in special education; (2) why they referred students for evaluation for placement in special education; and (3) their opinions about students based on gender, race/ethnicity, and/or socioeconomic background. Therefore, you need to

CHART 4.1 Demographics Related to Teachers Who Had Referred Students for Evaluation for Special Education by Grade Level in District A.

Grade Level	Total Number	Percent with Credits	Average Credits	Average Years Teaching	Gender		
					Male	Female	N/A
Elementary	22	36%	9	20.6	1	18	3
Middle school	13	31%	11	17.6	4	9	0
High school	8	13%	10	13.3	3	4	1

develop a profile of classroom teachers who referred students for evaluation for placement in special education as a first step to determine whether the referral process is equitable, objective, and efficient.

You need to identify the type of teacher that refers students for evaluation for special education in order to determine if age, gender, experience, or education influences decisions to refer students for evaluation for placement in special education. Only teachers can provide you with this information because districts do not keep records of this nature. To obtain this information, teachers need to be surveyed. Surveys ask for information about the teacher's gender, years of full-time teaching experience, and the number of credits that a teacher earned in special education courses (Chart 2.1). Remember, this type of information permits you to customize your staff development program to specific groups of classroom teachers based upon your findings.

Once you have the completed surveys, create a classroom teacher file in your database. First, place an identification number on each returned survey. This is meant to guarantee the anonymity and confidentiality of all participants, yet it allows you to cross-reference all data from the same form. If you have nine completed forms from classroom teachers the identification field will be one character wide. If there are ten to ninety-nine completed forms, the field will be two characters wide. Second, the field for school is two characters wide. Each school should be identified by a code beginning with 01, 02, . . . 99. Third, the field for grade should be two characters wide, that is, PK, K, 01, . . . 12. Fourth, the field for gender should be two characters wide. This permits you to total and/or average the number of female and/or male teachers

that referred students. Fifth, the field for years of full-time teaching should be three characters wide. This permits you to total and/or average the experience of classroom teachers. Sixth, the field for the number of credits earned in special education should be three characters wide. This will permit you to total and/or average the number of credits earned in special education by classroom teachers.

ILLUSTRATION: PROFILE OF CLASSROOM TEACHERS WHO HAD REFERRED STUDENTS FOR EVALUATION FOR PLACEMENT IN SPECIAL EDUCATION

The database helps to identify relationships between these variables. In one study where 107 teachers completed the survey, and in another study where 88 teachers completed the survey, it was found that a greater percent of those who referred students had earned university credits in special education courses and earned more credits than those who had not referred students. You should put this information in a chart. Chart 4.1 provides a profile for District A where forty-three out of 107 classroom teachers referred students by grade level, while Chart 4.2 provides information about District B where seventy out of eighty-eight classroom teachers referred students for placement for special education.

Remember, not all classroom teachers complete all questions related to demographic information. Some do not identify their gender for political reasons. Others do not identify their school or grade level/subject because they think this information will identify them and

CHART 4.2 Demographics Related to Teachers Who Had Referred Students for Evaluation for Special Education by Grade Level in District B.

Grade Level	Total Number	Percent with Credits	Average Years Teaching	Gender	
				Male	Female
Elementary	62	26%	23.5	6	54
Middle school	3	33%	17.3	3	0
High school	5	20%	23.6	2	3

Three teachers did not indicate the grade level they taught or the school in which they taught. These were teachers 01, 22, and 57.

present a problem for them. In cases where there is one class on a grade level, the identity of the classroom teacher could be compromised if one was not circumspect in the presentation of information.

ILLUSTRATION: NUMBER OF STUDENTS REFERRED FOR PLACEMENT

The database you created for students provides you with information about the number of students referred by grade, by gender, by race/ethnicity, and by family status. You can estimate that 70% to 75% of students referred for evaluation will come from the preschool and elementary grades, and 25% to 30% will come from secondary school.

Grade	Number of Students (large district)	Number of Students (average district)
PS	12	28
K	62[1]	7
P1	8	0
1	40	10
2	35	11
3	38	9
4	24	8
5	30	6
6	20	4
7	24	5
8	19	5
9	24	3
10	18	7
11	18	0
12	9	2
SE	1	

One interesting phenomenon that I found in the audits I implemented is that the percent of males compared to females referred for evaluation for special education decrease from elementary school to high school. In one large district, females made up 30% of students referred in elementary school and 46% of students referred in secondary school. In one average size district, females made up 39% of students referred in elementary school and 43% of students referred in secondary school. Another interesting point is that, in both districts, approximately two-thirds of the students that transferred into the program from other districts were males. Remember, you want information about the number and classification of transfer students and the schools from which they transferred. This will help

[1]Keep in mind that some or all of these students had been referred for placement before they entered kindergarten.

you identify districts with whom you need to establish better communications so that records are forwarded quickly to you and information about their special education curriculum is available to you. Also, you need to know whether there are different patterns that exist regarding referrals of local and transfer students.

BOILERPLATE: TRANSFER STUDENTS

Here is a boilerplate to use to write this portion of your summative report:

The percent of males compared to females referred for evaluation for special education decreases from elementary school to high school. Females made up 30% of students referred in elementary school and 46% of students referred in secondary school. Included in these figures were the 146 transfer students referred for evaluation for special education. Eventually, sixty-nine were classified LD, thirty-three were classified ED, eighteen were classified SI, eleven were classified MH, five were classified OHI, two were classified OI, one was classified MR, four were not classified and three moved. Eighty-nine (61%) of the transfer students were males, and fifty-seven (39%) were females. Fifty-four (37%) students were from nuclear families, and ninety-two (63%) were from nonnuclear families. Twenty-six (17.8%) were minority students, and forty (27.3%) students received free or reduced lunch.

LOCALLY WRITTEN CRITERIA

Every time a child is referred for evaluation for placement in special education, it requires the time of the professional staff and money. When the child truly needs special education services, these are resources well used; however, when the child does not need to be classified, money and time are wasted at a time when both are scarce. It costs approximately $1300–$2000 to evaluate a student for placement in special education. This includes the time needed by pupil personnel services to administer and evaluate tests, observe the child, and meet with parents. Unless classroom teachers know the criteria for placement of students in special education, they cannot be expected to make an informed judgment as to whether a child meets the criteria for placement. Unless members of pupil personnel services have a criteria in place, they cannot ensure the school community that the same criteria are applied to all students, regardless of gender, race/ethnicity, and/or socioeconomic status. Unless CSE members use criteria, they cannot ensure the school community that the decision-making process is equitable for all students.

In virtually every school district in which an audit was implemented, district personnel used state regulations as criteria for the evaluation of students for placement in special education. These regulations are not criteria, but guidelines. They are vague, especially as they relate to classification of learning disabled and emotionally handicapped students. Your district needs to spell out criteria in order to ensure that the same standards are applied to all students, regardless of gender, race/ethnicity, and/or socioeconomic status. Rarely are there locally written criteria in place for all categories of classification. Sometimes, there are locally written criteria to evaluate if kindergarten students are learning disabled, and sometimes, there are criteria in place to evaluate if students are speech impaired, but I have never seen locally written criteria for all classifications for all students. Although most classroom teachers, special education teachers, principals, psychologists, and CSE members indicate that they know the local criteria for student placement in special education in every audit, there were CSE members, principals, special education teachers, and regular classroom teachers who had not seen any locally written criteria for student placement in special education.

ILLUSTRATION: ANECDOTAL COMMENTS ABOUT LOCALLY WRITTEN CRITERIA FOR CLASSIFICATION OF STUDENTS

Those people who stated that there are locally written criteria in place normally identify state guidelines as the criteria or specify the method or process followed for classification of students. The most common answers given to the question about what were the local written criteria for student placement in special education are

- that it was either consistent with or was found in the regulations of the commissioner of education
- that it called for a 50% discrepancy between a student's achievement and potential on standardized tests and on an individual basis for learning disabled and emotionally handicapped classifications
- that it required that the child scores below 25% in two or more areas of language in order to qualify as speech impaired

Other people describe the method and/or process used to classify students. They point out that they use a

discrepancy level chart prepared by Robert T. and William J. Smith to determine if a child is functioning at a level 50% below what might be expected of a child of the same age and IQ. Additionally, we use the

Stanford Diagnostics and usually find our LD population scoring two years below grade level. . . . There is no one method of assessing learning disabilities; or IQ tests, standardized tests, diagnostic testing, formal and informal teacher observations, classroom functioning, report cards, teacher progress reports and recommendations.

You will find that another group of people will cite specific behaviors and/or factors as criteria for placement of students in special education. These include

- the failure of the student to meet the standard reference point (SRP) on tests
- the student's poor classroom performance
- the failure of remediation efforts to improve student outcomes
- the failure of student retention to improve the student's performance
- formal and informal assessment by resource room teachers and the psychologist
- how quickly a child is able to learn
- all building intervention techniques having been exhausted prior to testing
- whether academic deficits significantly hinder classroom performance

What is even more important for you to consider is that the source of information for classroom teachers, CSE members, and parents about the criteria for student placement in special education comes mainly from special education personnel and pupil personnel staff. Those who are most often the source of information are special education administrators and teachers, psychologists, speech therapists, social workers, and resource room teachers and, at the elementary school level, principals. Remember, the fact that detailed written criteria are not in place, much less distributed to faculty and staff, make it difficult for staff to develop parameters for referrals. Also, the fact that many people involved in the process are uninformed about the criteria for student placement in special education raises questions about the integrity and objectivity of the participants in the referral process. Is one a cynic to think that the fox has been asked to guard the chickenhouse?

Before you go any further, check to see whether your district has written criteria for placement of students in special education. Determine whether your staff is well versed in the criteria for student placement in special education.

PROBLEMS/DIFFICULTIES THAT TRIGGER REFERRALS

You need to know the reasons why classroom teachers refer students for evaluation for special education to either validate that the reasons are sound, to take steps to educate classroom teachers about valid reasons, and/or to determine if specific reasons are related to specific gender, race/ethnic, and/or socioeconomic groups. You will find that there are four major reasons for referrals given by classroom teachers. They are

(1) The inability of a student to function academically within the classroom norm
(2) Social and emotional difficulties that impede learning
(3) Speech, articulation, language, auditory, perceptual problems
(4) A student's chronic frustration

Other reasons cited include attention deficit disorder (ADD), attention deficit hyperactivity disorder (ADHD), and drugs or alcohol use by student or parent.

Remember, there is nothing inherently faulty with these reasons, nor do they imply that there is any bias on the part of the teacher nor any institutional bias; however, you need to assure yourself that specific reasons are not used to characterize a specific group of students and for certainty of the equity and objectivity of the process. Also, you need to know whether classroom teachers want information and strategies to help students in class or if they want to have students removed from class.

STEPS TO REMEDIATE PROBLEMS

You need to know what classroom teachers do to help students overcome their difficulties in class in order to form a sound judgment about whether a student needs to be placed in a more restrictive environment. Usually classroom teachers take steps to assist students with difficulties/problems before (prereferral) students are referred for evaluation for placement in special education. More often than not, teachers try more than one approach to help students before they refer students for evaluation for placement in special education. However, the six steps that are most frequently taken by teachers to assist students prior to referral are, in descending order, to

- notify and consult with parents
- provide students with individualized instruction
- discuss the situation with special education personnel, psychologists, guidance counselors, and/or social workers
- refer students for remedial assistance
- review the situation with the principal
- use a behavior modification strategy with students

Remember, teachers need to be educated about the steps to take to remediate problems and difficulties, especially teachers new to your district/school. You might want to provide classroom teachers with a list of steps to take to remediate problems and difficulties, and you might want to have an inservice program dedicated to this subject.

PURPOSE FOR REFERRALS

Normally, when asked, classroom teachers give at least one of three major reasons for the referral of students for evaluation. First, the lion's share of classroom teachers' comments indicate that they refer students because they think that special education programs are a more appropriate placement for students, that special education programs better serve the needs of students, and that special education programs help students succeed—that is, they get the best out of students and help students to function better in society. Second, classroom teachers indicate that they hope to gain information and insights about students and strategies to help those students in their classrooms. In one audit, a teacher wrote that her purpose was "to diagnose the problem and learn how the child might be better helped, so that he/she may achieve to his/her fullest potential." Third, a small group of classroom teachers indicate that they want students removed from their classroom for the greater good of all students.

It is interesting to note special education personnel have their own impressions as to why classroom teachers refer students for evaluation for placement in special education. These reasons cover the entire continuum, that is, from wanting information about students to removal of students from class. In one audit, special education teachers painted a picture of a continuum of perceptions that ranged from sincere concern to callous indifference on the part of classroom teachers. One special education teacher wrote, "Unfortunately many [classroom teachers] just want to get students out of their environment"; another said some classroom teachers want "to reduce their own responsibility and workload"; and classroom teachers "are not interested in intervention techniques or strategies that can be utilized by them in the classroom."

Remember, the reasons for referrals affects the integrity of the special education program. Unless students who are truly handicapped are placed in the program, the program is contaminated. It is possible that bothersome students and/or students who perform poorly in class are not handicapped.

ROLE OF SPECIAL EDUCATION PERSONNEL IN THE REFERRAL PROCESS

There is no doubt that special education personnel have a strategic role in decisions by teachers to refer students for evaluation for special education. You need to determine whether they have had too great an influence on decisions made by classroom teachers to refer students for evaluation for placement in special education. You need to know whether special education personnel are honest brokers or seducers. Are they people, collectively, who want to help teachers deal with students with problems/difficulties in the classroom, or are they interested in expanding the enrollment of the special education program?

Special education personnel are consulted as problems arise, observe students, suggest strategies, test students, and debrief classroom teachers. The key role played by special education personnel in the referral process is gleaned from comments from classroom teachers:

- I have consulted with all of them before referring a child so I could get their input and to determine if a child would qualify for services.
- On any occasion when I thought a referral might be a possibility, I touch base with each of the above professional staff, in addition to special area teachers. The input and support of those people is of major importance to me in making sure the student's needs will be met.
- They guided any approach in handling placement for referring students for evaluation.
- These people, after much thought, testing, and past experience, can make the judgment as to the proper placement of a child in difficulty.
- The personnel in my building guide me and consult with me in reaching the necessary decisions regarding the student with special needs.
- Sometimes, they have suggested a referral based on previous years' work; in our discussions, they have guided and assisted in the referral.
- I personally consult with resource room teachers (and sometimes other special education personnel) before making any decisions about possible referrals and for prereferral intervention suggestions.
- They play an important role in the decision. The special education personnel guide and inform us. Our questions are answered and group decisions are valuable. Testing is done, and results are discussed.
- I generally discuss the child with the appropriate specialist before referring to ascertain his/her opinion as to whether the referral is appropriate.

One has to question whether special education personnel and especially school psychologists are then too close to an individual case to be able to make a decision on the placement of a student and whether the roles of factfinder/analyzer and decision maker should rest with separate bodies of people. Remember, psychologists may low key their influence over classroom teachers. They point out that they are part of a multidisciplinary team. Their role is to consult with teachers and parents and administrators to discuss intervention strategies and possible alternatives to CSE referrals. On the other hand, special education teachers oftentimes indicate that they play a significant role in the referral process. One special education teacher wrote that she was a ''member of the Building Team. I am part of the referral process as we meet to discuss children who exhibit difficulties within the classroom. I participate in the decision to test, I test children, and participate in the decision to place the child in resource room.''

ROLE OF THE BUILDING ADMINISTRATOR IN TEACHERS' REFERRALS OF STUDENTS

It is common knowledge that, for a program to be successful, the building principal needs to show support and be directly responsible for supervising the program. You need to know the degree to which principals take responsibility for the management and operation of the special education program in their buildings. If you are a principal, you need to take an honest look at your role in the management and operation of your special education program. More specifically, you need to know the degree to which principals monitor and assist teachers in the prereferral and referral processes.

You will find that there are perceptual differences between classroom teachers and principals about the role of principals in the initial phases of the referral process and the assistance that the principal provides in the referral process to classroom teachers. Usually, classroom teachers, especially elementary classroom teachers, point out that principals have an important role in the prereferral and referral process. However, do not be surprised if your principals indicate that they play an insignificant role in the prereferral and referral process. In our audits, we have found that, generally, classroom teachers term principals supportive, note the principals' positive role in developing strategies for placing children, point out that principals encourage prereferral intervention, and note that they review the referral form. You can get the flavor by classroom teacher comments:

- He encourages us to try all possible means of intervention before a child is referred. He participates in team meetings to monitor progress. He participates in the decision-making process.

- He has been a great help to me in referrals. He knows all the laws and shares his knowledge with the staff on this and all matters; conducts weekly team meetings.
- He helped develop a strategy for placing children or helped with contact with child's parents.
- The building principal has helped by suggesting the path to take to refer a student.
- The building principal has asked for prereferral intervention and wants to see these as well as the final referral form.
- He usually reviews the first copy and discusses any concerns he might have about the referral before it is typed and presented to the parent for acceptance.
- Principals indicated that their involvement in the referral process varied from hardly any involvement to weekly meetings.

Remember, effective principals set the climate and expectation for their schools and programs, including special education. Our audits have indicated that, when principals take an active interest in the special education process and program, classroom teachers are more apt to exhaust all methods and strategies to remediate problems and difficulties before they refer students for evaluation for special education.

REFERRALS BY GENDER

It is common knowledge that special education nationally is virtually a private school for males, minorities, and the poor. Although it is relatively easy to determine if there are disproportionate numbers of males, minorities, and poor students in your special education program, it is more difficult to determine the reason for this pattern in your district/school. However, the most effective and efficient way to shed light on this problem for your district/school is to scrutinize all referrals from the past academic year and listen to the comments made by classroom teachers, special education teachers, principals, psychologists, social workers, and CSE members.

BOILERPLATE: PRESENTATION OF INFORMATION BY GENDER

First, use the special education files in your district to get the information needed for your student database. The district files should tell you the student's identification number, name, gender, status, and current classification. Here is a boilerplate to use to write this portion of your summative report.

During the academic year, there were 3180 students enrolled in the school district. District data indicates that there were 1649 males (52%) and 1531 females (48%) enrolled in the school district. In this period, 106 students were referred for evaluation for special education. Of the 106 students, sixty-four (60%) were males and forty-two (40%) were females. Eventually, 50% (53) of the students referred were classified LD. Twenty-eight of these students were males and twenty-five were females. Eventually, 22% (23) were classified SI. Sixteen of these students were males and seven were females. Eventually, 14% (15) were classified ED. Eleven of these students were males and four were females. Eventually, 8% (8) were classified MH. Five of these students were females and three were males. Eventually, 1% (1) was classified MR. The student was a male. Six students (6%) were not classified. Five of the students were males and one was a female.

Second, after you have determined whether there are more males than females referred for evaluation for placement in special education in your district, you can ask classroom teachers, special education teachers, principals, social workers, psychologists, and CSE members to explain this phenomenon. The responses in our audits raise some serious concerns about (1) sexism in the referrals of males for placement in special education, (2) the slighting of females because of their quietness and/or passivity in class, and (3) the appropriateness of the mainstream curriculum.

There are many comments that indicate that there are genetic/developmental reasons for a greater number of males than females referred for special education. And yet one wonders whether boys are handicapped or victims of a curriculum and/or teaching style that rewards quietness and passivity and punishes boisterousness and aggressiveness. More importantly, classroom teachers, special education teachers, social workers, and CSE members suggest that the learning environment is a contributing cause for the large number of males referred for special education. In our audits, these professionals suggest that the large number of male referrals may be due to a curriculum that rewards passivity, a class environment that discourages movement, and teaching styles that do not match student learning styles.

Here are some sample answers to let you know the thoughts of school faculty on the large and/or disproportionate number of males referred for evaluation for placement in special education. These sample comments raise questions regarding the appropriateness of referrals for males who are on the correct developmental track for males. Faculty members thought

- Male babies are born more at risk for all difficulties.

- From what I have read, several medical conditions that require special education services affect more males than females, for example, spina bifida, ADD.
- There may be a genetic predisposition for learning disabilities for males.
- Females are born with less birth defects.
- Genetics plays an important role in learning disorders and emotionally inherited conditions, for example, ADHD is more common in boys than girls.
- The male nervous system is less well developed at birth; therefore, it takes several years for him to catch up to the female maturation process. If a problem exists, it shows more quickly in a male. Males carry and show more genetic problems than females do.
- Statistics reveal that more males are born with developmental delays than females. Many syndromes that occur with learning disabilities are more predominant in males than in females.
- As sexist as this sounds, I do not feel the home and school fully recognize that boys are typically slower to develop than girls.
- Differences in central nervous system, differences in processing of information, differences in learning modalities, more immaturity in males, and different expectations account for the greater percent of males in special education.
- Learning difficulties appear more significant in males because ADD seems to affect them more.
- Males are developmentally behind females in the primary area.
- Males are developmentally immature at younger ages.
- A male's slower rate of maturation could lead to learning difficulties.
- Boys are developmentally more delayed and not as ready for the formal academic challenges.
- Male maturity rate is slower. Their immaturity interferes with their learning.
- Males tend to mature more slowly than females and may act out due to frustration more than females.
- Males are less mature at certain age levels than females. Males are missing one (1) X chromosome, which may help mask or compensate for learning problems.
- Research and statistics have shown that the male population seemed to exhibit greater weaknesses in reading acquisition and to have a greater incidence of LD.

Other faculty members suggest that societal factors are

the reason more males than females are referred for placement in special education. Here are some sample comments:

- Males tend to be more active and vocal, and it is easier to detect problem areas as opposed to girls who are more quiet and reserved.
- Boys tend to be more aggressive and more active. Quiet students (girls) might be overlooked until they are older (4, 5, 6 grade).
- Boys are looked upon as being more aggressive in behavior, etc. Girls are more focused at the start of school years and aim to please.
- Boys tend to be more active and therefore gain attention more easily. They are more apt to be distracted from work they find difficult.
- Females present more passive problems. Males are more easily identified since they are more inclined to physically demonstrate their needs.
- Boys tend to act out their emotional problems in a physical way. Girls tend to use their mouths to act out. Girls will try to avoid confrontation.
- Females are pushed in our society to be more submissive. Concurrently, males are allowed to be more aggressive which becomes a problem in a teaching environment.
- Referrals are sometimes inspired by, not only poor achievement, but poor effort, irresponsible work habits, and poor social behavior (distracting others).
- Referrals occur with greater frequency at primary grades. Primary grades must deal with boys who reveal their disabilities in a more overt acting out manner. The squeaky wheel gets the grease.
- Males tend to demand more attention under duress. Especially in primary schools, the institution is dominated by females. Gender issues impact relationships.
- Males tend to be more of a discipline problem. Too many times, male students are referred for special education because of discipline and not educational reasons. They should be dealt with by the administration, thus focusing the attention on the students who truly deserve special education referral.
- Boys will more frequently act out causing disruptions to the entire class. The frustration from academics is often linked to poor behaviors; it would be more beneficial to the child to assess their needs to see if a disability is present.
- When males are experiencing difficulty in the

classroom, they tend to act out more than girls, who generally tend to keep to themselves hoping they will not be noticed as having difficulties. When a child acts out, teachers refer them for testing more quickly.

- Unfortunately, many males are still more vocal and act inappropriately in class when they are having difficulties.
- Boys usually have greater difficulty adjusting to a classroom atmosphere.
- Females at a young age may be more introverted, less likely to exhibit "red flags" to a teacher.
- More males are referred, possibly due to inappropriate behaviors displayed by the child, which teachers may not be able to handle.
- Boys have a tendency to "act out" behaviorally — more than girls — also, gender bias.

Always a handful of faculty members suggest that the problem may rest with the regular/mainstream curriculum. They think that

- Too much is expected at too early an age. Many boys need a more "hands-on" program enriched with science and activities where they can get up and move about. The curriculum is heavy with many reading and writing activities that "young" boys can't fulfill.
- Males reach developmental levels at a different pace than females. Some of these children might benefit by beginning kindergarten at a later time (screening will help identify these children).
- The school environment may not provide the appropriate learning styles needed by males to reach their potential.
- Males exhibit more impulsive and aggressive behaviors than females. Teaching styles and materials are geared more towards quiet seat work — developmental differences.
- There is a tendency of schools to teach using skills that are geared more toward female (so-called) interests and aptitudes. Also, there is a preponderance of female elementary teachers.
- Males who are experiencing difficulty with the curriculum will usually stand out more because their behavior is negatively affected.

REFERRALS BY STUDENT'S FAMILY STATUS

You need to know the family background of classified students in your district/school to determine if there are disproportionate numbers of classified children from single-parent/foster households and whether the program meets the needs of these students. In our audits, we found that these children make up between 33% and 41% of the students referred for evaluation for placement in special education. Remember, because most referred students are in elementary school, any family tragedy such as death, illness, and divorce is no more than a year or two in their past. In the course of our audits we came across more than a handful of children whose both parents and a sibling had died of AIDS. There were children whose parents died of a lingering illness. And there were scores of children whose father's or mother's whereabouts were unknown. You need to know whether these children need to be classified and placed in a class to improve their academic performance or need professional psychiatric help unavailable at schools to grieve, cope, and deal with their understandable pain that is time limited. You need to know whether suggestions by special education personnel to parents/guardians that these children be placed in special education are because these children are, in fact, handicapped or to take advantage of people that are vulnerable and/or poorly educated in order to increase the number of children in the program.

One of the problems in dealing with this topic is that school districts usually do not have data regarding their students' family status. So there is no way to determine whether there is a disproportionate number of students from single-parent households referred and classified. Also, there is not any data available to indicate the number of students from single-parent/guardian households in honor, gifted, and regular programs to make comparisons. Finally, there are no data for neighboring schools or schools in your state to use as a comparison. However, data from your district/school/program do shed light on your unique situation and permit you to determine the equity and objectivity of the referral process.

BOILERPLATE: PRESENTATION OF INFORMATION BY FAMILY STATUS

In all likelihood, you will need to get information about a student's family status from the special education file. This information should be included in the social worker's background report or on the referral form filed by the classroom teacher or in the psychological report. However, do not be too surprised if this information is omitted from all these reports for a number of students. Once you have this information, enter it in to the student database.

Here are two examples of a boilerplate to use to write this portion of your summative report.

Example 1: Of the 106 students referred for special education, seventy-one (67%) were from a nuclear family and thirty-five (33%) were from single-parent households. Eventually, twenty-one of these students from single-parent households were classified LD, nine were classified ED, and three were classified MH. None of these students were classified SI. Two students were not classified. Twenty-one of these students were males and fourteen were females.

Example 2: Of the 382 students referred for special education, information on family status was unavailable for twenty-nine (8%) students. Of the remaining 353 students, 207 (59%) were from a nuclear family and 146 (41%) were from single-parent households. Eventually, fifty-eight (40%) of these students from single-parent households were classified LD, forty-seven (32%) were classified ED, twenty-three (16%) were classified SI, eight (5%) were classified MH, six (4%) were classified OHI, one (1%) was classified OI, and one (1%) was classified MR. Seven (5%) students from single-parent households were not classified. Three students (2%) that withdrew or moved were from single-parent households. Eighty-nine males and fifty-seven females were from single-parent/foster family households.

You will find that the lion's share of classroom teachers, special education teachers, psychologists, principals, and CSE members are aware of the growth of single-parent households in the country and in your district and that they know of many students from single-parent households that function well in school. They tend to empathize with the plight of students and parents in a single-parent household. Their comments provide insights of the obstacles in the way of real program reform as well as reasons that students from single-parent households are apt to be referred for evaluation. Comments that indicate that they understand the societal and individual dimensions of the problem but do not question the appropriateness of such referrals include

- I feel very strongly about this topic. I see the family unit disappearing more and more. There is little structure in homes, less quality time spent together, too little reading and too much television.
- Because of the proportionally higher number of single families, I would believe that a large percentage of all our families are single-parent ones so the percent here is not as disproportionate as first glance may suggest.
- I'm not sure what this statistic tells us since

56% of students referred for special education come from ''complete family/parent situations.''
- Many children having handicapping conditions have special needs. These needs create stress which many marriages may not survive.
- Sometimes, when parents are faced with a difficult child/handicap, it creates undue stress, which then, in turn, causes the family to split.
- Many children with disabilities have behaviors that can (may) cause tremendous distress in parents, which may cause a higher rate of separation.
- I am from a single-parent family. From what I remember, it was a living hell being torn between Mom and Dad. Today's children have it worse. . . . [Parents are] not around when the children need them.

On the other hand, classroom teachers, special education teachers, principals, social workers, psychologists, and CSE members express deep concern, knowledge, and empathy with the deprivations experienced by some children who live in a single-parent household; suggest some negative effects it has on a student's schooling; and hint at the inappropriateness of referrals. Samples of their comments include:

- Children with a single parent have more to cope with. Their parent may be overwhelmed by work and child care and not have enough time for the child or be angry and abrupt due to all the stress in his/her life. Plus, emotionally, it's hard to concentrate on school while grieving for the absent parent and feeling less secure in a changing family.
- This trauma is transmitted to the child and affects every aspect of his life and learning.
- Perhaps the parent does not have time to work with the child at home, thus magnifying the learning disability.
- The child may not be well supervised after school hours. There may be little or no monitoring of school progress.
- Parent involvement in school success is important. Single-parent homes may be busy working to support the family and don't have the time to devote to helping the student.
- Single parents are at a disadvantage timewise with helping their children and to compensate for learning problems.
- Less supervision is common with regard to study habits, homework, organization, and discipline.
- There is no doubt that one's emotional state is directly related to all facets of one's life—especially the learning process.

- Time to help the child with school work may be minimal or nonexistent. Emotional factors from the situation may affect the student.
- Not receiving the necessary academic support from home with studying or homework and their poor work is more apparent because there is less parental checking of work.
- There is less time for a single parent to help his/her child with homework. Also, there is probably less money to spend on extras, such as computers or trips to a museum.
- These children have so much on their minds that they don't consider education a priority.
- They may need counseling because of the home situation; academic difficulties can be tied to emotional problems.
- The situation is devastating to a child and is greatly expressed through a child's behavior and educational performance.
- Most of these children may not be receiving the support they need at home to increase their academic skills and understanding. They are doing homework independently and have other ''emotional'' problems that may interfere with their learning.
- There can be many reasons, some social, some psychological, some academic. Much of the single parenting that is being done is done by women, who are traditionally paid lower wages and are victims of nonsupport. School issues pale by comparison when many are scratching out an existence. Time isn't there to help.
- There is not as much time available in the home

for supporting the child who needs extra assistance to master concepts.
- Single parents have more difficulty providing additional educational guidance needed for learning disabled students.
- Single parents don't have the time to devote what is needed to a special education child, especially if they have other children and are working.
- Typically, a single parent may work longer hours, and these children perhaps do not get the academic support and reinforcement they need at home in order to ensure successful educational experiences.
- Without the ability to access established prereferral services, there are no options.
- Children are at risk for learning problems and social emotional difficulty due to family stress.

SUMMARY

Remember, the purpose of this chapter was to give you an overview of the referral process, provide you with practical and usable information about the referral process gathered from audits, and show you how to go about the process to ensure the equity, objectivity, and effectiveness of this aspect of the management and operation of special education. The next step is to apply this information and process to referred students who were eventually classified LD, SI, or ED. This process helps you surgically target areas in the prereferral and referral stages so that you can downsize your special program.

5

Six Steps to Reduce the Number of Referrals of Students Eventually Classified Learning Disabled

AIM

THIS chapter shows you six steps to take to reduce the number of students referred for evaluation for placement in special education, who eventually are classified LD. There are charts and examples to help you see how variables such as the student's gender, terms and phrases used by classroom teachers, the intelligence range of students, student's grade level, and the family status of students influence the referral of students who eventually are classified LD. You will learn how to piece together subtleties and nuances in the referral process that pervert the intention of special education and undermine the integrity of the LD classification. Snapshots of the referral process gathered by the method spelled out in this chapter help you develop more specific/meaningful LD criteria for the referral of students. You will be able to devise a customized quality control mechanism for your school/district to better ensure that only those students who truly need services are referred. That is a first step to placing a lid on the proliferation of special education programs.

REFERRALS OF STUDENTS WHO WERE EVENTUALLY CLASSIFIED LEARNING DISABLED

Although it should not surprise you that the majority of students referred for evaluation eventually are classified LD, it might cause you to question the appropriateness of this classification once you have a series of pictures of referred students who eventually are classified LD. You can determine whether these referrals are appropriate or inappropriate. If inappropriate, you will be able to determine if there is either gender, racial/ethnic, and/or socioeconomic bias in the referral and classification of students or a district/school mentality that encourages the referral and classification of demanding/bothersome students or an ethos that encourages the referral of failing students.

In the audits that I implemented, I found that the lion's share of students grades K – 12 referred for special education are eventually classified LD. The definition of an LD student throughout the United States is basically similar to that of New York State. In New York State, the regulations of the commissioner of education defines learning disabled as

> A pupil with a disorder in one or more of the basic psychological processes involved in understanding or in using language, spoken or written, which manifests itself in an imperfect ability to listen, think, speak, read, write, spell, or to do mathematical calculations.

> The term includes such conditions as perceptual handicaps, brain injury, neurological impairment, minimal brain dysfunction, dyslexia and developmental aphasia. The term does not include children who have learning problems which are primarily the result of visual, hearing or motor handicaps, or mental retardation, of emotional disturbance, or of environmental, cultural or economic disadvantage. A child who exhibits a discrepancy of 50 percent or more between expected achievement and actual achievement determined on an individual basis shall be deemed to have a learning disability.

But keep in mind that the New York State Commissioner's Office has determined that the

> 50% discrepancy standard is to be used as a guideline in making a qualitative assessment of the child's ability and achievement; it is not to be applied as a quantitative formula. The Department will consider the use of a 50% discrepancy formula as a compliance violation.

Before you implement the steps spelled out in this chapter, you need to keep in mind that Gartner and Lipsky (1987, p.373) identified five issues that raised questions about the operational definition of the LD label. There was concern about

(1) The excessive numbers of students classified LD

(2) The vagueness of the term so that more than 80% of students could be classified LD by definitions used

(3) The inability of experienced evaluators to distinguish between students who were LD and those who were not

(4) The inability to distinguish LD students from other low achievers with regard to a wide variety of school-related characteristics

(5) A Colorado study that indicated that more than half the children did not meet statistical or valid clinical criteria for the definition of perceptual or communicative disorders

The authors noted that these concerns were due to "reports concerning the inadequacy and inappropriateness of the measuring instruments, the disregard of results in decision making, and, often, the evaluators' incompetence and biasness."

REFERRALS BY GENDER

In order to analyze the referrals in your district/school, you need to use the database file you created for students. First, index the database by grade level of students. This means that the reports generated will list students by grade level, in ascending order, that is, all first graders followed by second graders. Second, have your database program provide you with a count of students who were referred for evaluation between July 1, 19XX and June 30, 19XX of the preceding academic year by eventual classification. Third, have your database program provide you with a count of females and males that were referred for evaluation between July 1, 19XX and June 30, 19XX of the preceding academic year by eventual classification. Fourth, have your database program provide you with a count of the intelligence range of students by gender that were referred for evaluation between July 1, 19XX and June 30, 19XX of the preceding academic year by eventual classification. You need to know the number of students by LD classification that were in the superior, high average, average, low average, borderline, and mentally deficient intelligence range. Fifth, have your database program provide you with a count of transfer students by gender that were referred for evaluation between July 1, 19XX and June 30, 19XX of the preceding academic year by eventual classification. Now you have all the hard data needed to develop a skeletal album of snapshots about the equity, objectivity, and effectiveness of the referral process. Also, you have information to determine the steps that you need to take to better supervise and monitor the referral process—a first step to reduce costs for the evaluation of students for placement in special education. Remember, this method also is used continuously to monitor the referral process in the current academic year.

ILLUSTRATION: REFERRAL OF STUDENTS EVENTUALLY CLASSIFIED LD BY GENDER

With hard data generated by the database program you can create a picture of the number and gender of students referred for special education who eventually will be classified LD. Moreover, you can clarify the impact that transfer students have on the size and therefore on the cost of the program. Two illustrations point out the magnitude of the issue.

Sample 1

In one audit 147 (38%) of the 382 students referred for evaluation for special education placement were eventually classified learning disabled. Ninety-one (62%) were males and fifty-six (38%) were females. The report that I wrote noted that

236 of the 382 students referred for evaluation for special education placement were initial referrals and 146 students were transfer students. Thirty-three percent of the 236 initial referrals were eventually classified LD. Forty-seven percent of the 146 transfer students were classified LD. In other words the transfer students increased the percent of students who were eventually classified LD.

Sixty-two percent of the students referred for evaluation and eventually classified LD were males and 38% were females. The transfer students had a slightly higher percent of females (39% to 37%) and slightly fewer males (63% to 61%) eventually classified LD than the group of students that were initial referrals.

Sample 2

A more detailed report that I wrote for another audit where 106 students had been referred for evaluation for placement in special education found

In all grades, except PS, K, 6, 10, and 12 the lion's share of students referred for special education were eventually classified LD. In PS and GRADE K the greatest number of students (13 out of 28 and 3 out of 7 respectively) were classified SI. In grades 6 and 10 an equal number of students (2 and 3 respectively) were classified ED.

Fifty-three students (50%) of the 106 students referred for evaluation for special education placement were eventually classified LD. Twenty-eight (53%) were males and 25 (47%) were females.

It is important to note that 55 students had been referred for evaluation for special education placement, at least partially, because district staff and/or parents were concerned about their poor academic performance. Twenty-one of the 55 students (56%) were males and 24 students (44%) were females.

Eventually, of these fifty-five students, 40 (73%) were

classified as LD, 5 (9%) were classified as Emotionally Disturbed, 4 (7%) were classified as Speech Impaired, 2 (4%) were classified as Multi-Handicapped and 4 (7%) were not classified. Twenty-one of the 40 students (53%) classified as LD were males and 19 students (48%) were females.

Thirteen other students were eventually classified LD. Nine of these students were new entrants who had been in special education programs. Five of these students were males and 4 were females. Another female student had been evaluated for a full day special education placement. One male student had been referred for speech and language deficits and another male had been referred for articulation problems. One female student had been referred for speech and language deficits.

Both males (86%) and females (83%) were referred for academic underachievement. It is important to note that 10 high school students were referred for academic reasons. Seven were referred for academic underachievement and 3 were referred for failing classes.

STEP 1 TO REDUCE THE SIZE OF THE STUDENT POOL

The first step that you need to take to ensure the equity, objectivity, and effectiveness of the referral process for students who are eventually classified LD is to determine whether there are more males than females referred for evaluation. If there are more males than females, you need to determine if the reasons for the referrals are valid. If they are not valid, then you have identified a way to reduce the size of the pool of students that would be tested and classified.

TERMS USED TO REFER STUDENTS

In all the audits that I implemented, I never once came across comments made by classroom teachers in the referral process that had a districtwide standardized operational definition. Nor have I found that the terms or phrases used by classroom teachers in one school/district are exactly the same terms or phrases used by classroom teachers in other schools/districts. Usually, classroom teachers indicate that students have "difficulty" with anything from reading/phonics to following oral directions. Never is the word *difficulty* defined for the specific academic issue. Do you know whether the word is used to define student performance in comparison to expected achievement? Or is it used to define student performance in comparison to a class, state, or national norm? Remember, it is important to know the reasons teachers refer students for evaluation for placement in special education. This helps you to determine the equity, objectivity, and effectiveness of the referral process. You can then determine whether

the referral process is abused. You have information to question whether students are placed inappropriately and whether costs for evaluation of students can be reduced.

You will find that the sample comments made by classroom teachers can be grouped into four categories: "academic," "behavioral," "speech and language," and "other" comments. You need to examine mainly the "academic" comments to determine the reasons why students who eventually are classified LD are referred for special education. However, students who are referred for "behavioral," "speech and language," and "other" comments are also apt to be classified LD eventually. Keep in mind that the "academic" comments made by teachers in referrals of students for evaluation for placement in special education lack uniform standards, criteria, and operational definitions. Notwithstanding this, the terms are a true representation of terms used by the teachers in your district who refer students. It is recognized that these terms might be reorganized, but any restructuring of these terms would not alter the findings. However, it is clear that your school/district needs to develop standardized operational definitions of academic difficulties for teachers who refer students for evaluations.

ILLUSTRATION: "ACADEMIC" TERMS USED TO DESCRIBE STUDENTS WHO EVENTUALLY ARE CLASSIFIED LD

Chart 5.1 is a good illustration of the different "academic" terms or phrases used to describe "academic" reasons for the referral of students for evaluation for placement in special education and who are eventually classified LD. Chart 5.1 indicates the number of times each term or phrase was used for males and females. It is probable that more than one term or phrase is used to describe the "academic" problems of a student. Remember, these terms are gathered from referral forms completed by classroom teachers or from psychological reports and entered into the student database. Also, "behavioral," "speech and language," and "other" comments are used to refer students who are eventually classified LD. Finally, terms and phrases used to refer students vary from school to school and district to district.

Please note that Chart 5.1 indicates that A.1 Reading/phonetics difficulty (40), A.16 Difficulty following oral directions/understanding directions (38), A.19 Difficulty in all areas (24), and A.20 Short attention span (23) accounted for 63% of the academic reasons given for referrals of students for evaluation for placement in special education who eventually were classified LD. It is important to note that Ysseldyke, Algozzine, Slinn, and McGue (1982) concluded that

CHART 5.1 Terms Related to Academic Performance Used to Refer Students
for Placement in Special Education by Gender.

	Terms Used	Males	Females
A.	Academic		
A.1	Reading/phonetics difficulty	25	15
A.2	Comprehension, word attach skills, and retention of sight words difficulty	5	6
A.4	Difficulty with numbers		
A.6	Written language difficulty	3	2
A.7	Language arts difficulty	3	1
A.8	Difficulty with a variety of sentence forms	1	1
A.9	Difficulty with letter identification	1	
A.10	Reading, math, other	3	3
A.11	Difficulty in critical thinking	2	
A.12	Difficulty with fine motor skills	9	3
A.13	Other academic problems	5	6
A.14	Difficulty processing information	3	2
A.16	Difficulty following oral directions/understanding directions	27	11
A.17	Delay in cognitive ability	2	6

there was not a defensible system for differentiating low achieving students from learning disabled students.

STEP 2 TO REDUCE THE SIZE OF THE STUDENT POOL

The second step that you need to take to ensure the equity, objectivity, and effectiveness of the referral process for students who are eventually classified LD is to define terms such as *difficulty* and *problems* used by classroom teachers to refer students. Because of the vagueness of terms and phrases, the number of students referred for evaluation for placement in special education is inflated. You now have a second way to reduce the pool of students referred for evaluation and yet strengthen the integrity of the referral process.

SCHOOL PSYCHOLOGISTS AND THE ABILITY TO DIFFERENTIATE LOW-ACHIEVING STUDENTS FROM LEARNING DISABLED STUDENTS

In the audits that I completed, I found, time after time, that the comments of the school psychologists raised questions as to whether low-achieving students were being classified LD. In one district, school psychologists identified three characteristics of LD children.

(1) They have an average intelligence and a 50% deficit in a specific area—children demonstrate a 50% discrepancy between measured potential and achievement skills in one of seven areas.

(2) They achieve poorly due to neurological conditions, that is, discrepancy between intelligence and achievement levels.

(3) They demonstrate profiles of strengths and weaknesses that are consistent with language processing deficits, memory deficits, perceptual motor deficits, and/or visual-spatial organization deficits, which impact on specific learning skills.

The psychologists identified five characteristics of a low achieving student. Low-achieving students

(1) Do not perform at a level a teacher may expect

(2) Have weaknesses across the board

(3) May be achieving poorly due to factors such as poor intelligence

(4) Do not meet the 50% discrepancy criteria between expectations based on intelligence functioning and academic achievement—the profile of deficits are not specific to a specific learning disorder

(5) May function below level for reasons such as motivational and adjustment difficulties

In another district, the responses of the school psychologists included

- The distinction is often fuzzy. Thank goodness diagnostic measures utilized by the psychologist can help with the differentiation.

- A learning disabled student has a disability.
- The profile of a learning disabled student shows more discrepancies between different cognitive abilities.
- When a child has a flat intellectual profile or is functioning within expectation for their ability, they are low achieving, not learning disabled.
- Low-achieving students are functioning at expected levels based on ability. LD shows discrepancy in various abilities.
- The LD student has a discrepancy between cognitive abilities and academic functioning.
- Low-achieving students are functioning at expected levels; LD student profile indicates discrepancies between neurocognitive skills and achievement.
- There are variable discrepancies in cognitive abilities and academic abilities of LD students, and they have at least average potential, whereas a true slow learner does not show such variabilities and their potential is below average.

Remember, the research in this area indicates that there was not a defensible system for differentiating low-achieving students from LD students. And yet the psychologists involved in audits indicated with great authority that they could differentiate low-achieving students from LD students.

COMPETENCY OF SCHOOL PSYCHOLOGISTS

You need to be aware of the fact that there are questions raised about the competency and integrity of school psychologists that cannot be dismissed out of hand or on the basis of faith. In a lecture entitled "The Reform of Assessment Practices in Special Education: The California Experience" (1991), Dr. Richard A. Figueroa noted the rationale for removing IQ and possibly most psychometric tests in special education. He noted psychometric evidence of bias. Dr. Figueroa, professor of education, University of California at Davis, pointed out that there was misuse of the diagnostic process in special education. He wrote "that school psychologists test until they find the 'right' profile, the profile that verifies the referral for testing." Also, he pointed out that testing of children really constitutes a form of medical malpractice. He wrote that there

is a group of adults known as school psychologists who have no medical training but who routinely make "diagnostic" decisions about medical conditions such as Mental Retardation, Attention Deficit disorders and neurological impairments (e.g. Learning Disabilities) on the basis of psychometric test scores. Some have suggested that the consequences of this professional

activity are the wide national disparities in the prevalence rates for mild handicapping conditions. . . . I would suggest that a plausible reason for such discrepancies is the practice of medicine without a license in the public schools. Some are suggesting that this Medical Model, which "looks" for the disabilities in the child and not in the curriculum, or the instruction, or system, may be just as implicated as the tests.

STEP 3 TO REDUCE THE SIZE OF THE STUDENT POOL

The third step that you need to take to ensure the equity, objectivity, and effectiveness of the referral process for students who are eventually classified LD is to reduce the external and internal pressure on school psychologists to classify students. Moreover, you need to make sure that school psychologists understand the difficulties in differentiating low-achieving students, from LD students. You are apt to find that the more questions you ask school psychologists about the referrals of low-achieving students, the more school psychologists are apt to suggest more remediation strategies to classroom teachers, and fewer low-achieving students are apt to be referred for evaluation. This is another way to reduce the pool of students referred for evaluation who do not need to be classified formally in order to receive the services they need.

INTELLIGENCE RANGE: LOW ABILITY STUDENTS AND LD CLASSIFICATION

Questions about the competency and integrity of school psychologists can be minimized because the audit provides you with information about the intelligence range of students referred for evaluation for placement in special education who are eventually classified LD. Charts 5.2A and 5.2B each represent findings from different schools/districts. They are examples of the information that you can gather about the intelligence range of referred students who are eventually classified LD. They each raise questions as to whether approximately 40% of low-ability students are classified LD inappropriately. These examples suggest that one way to reduce costs and downsize the special education population is to make sure that low-achieving students are not classified LD.

Chart 5.2A indicates that 59% of all the students that were classified LD were at the average or above intelligence range when one includes only students for which intelligence data was available. This means that 41% of all students that were classified LD were at low average or below intelligence range. Does the percent of students in the low average or below intelligence range raise a red flag? Were low-achieving students

CHART 5.2A **Intelligence Range of Students Referred and Transfer Students Who Were Eventually Classified LD by Gender.**

Intelligence Range	Initially Classified Learning Disabled		Classified Transfers	
	Female	Male	Female	Male
Superior		1		1
High average	1	4	1	
Average	12	23	4	18
Low average	6	10	10	7
Borderline	1	1	2	6
Mentally deficient		1		1
N/A	9	9	9	10
	29	49	27	42

classified LD in this district? What effect does this have on human and financial resources earmarked for special education? What does this mean in terms of the integrity of the special education program?

Chart 5.2B indicates that 57% of all the referred students that are classified LD are at the average or above intelligence range. Chart 5.2B indicates that a greater percent of females (63%) than males (52%) with average and above intelligence range were eventually classified LD. However, when one includes only in district students and excludes transfer students, the picture changes. Columns 1 and 3 indicate that twenty-five out of thirty-one males (81%) and fifteen out of twenty-four females (63%) had an average and above intelligence range.

Four students referred for evaluation for placement in special education for academic reasons were not classified at all. All four students were males. Two of the students were in the superior and two were in the average intelligence range.

STEP 4 TO REDUCE THE SIZE OF THE STUDENT POOL

The fourth step that you need to take to ensure the equity, objectivity, and effectiveness of the referral process for students who are eventually classified LD

is to make sure that students at or below the "low average" intelligence range are not referred for evaluation for placement in special education by classroom teachers for "academic" reasons when these students are working up to their ability. This is another way to reduce the pool of students referred for evaluation who do not need to be classified formally in order to receive the services they need.

REFERRALS BY GRADE LEVEL: IS THE EDUCATIONAL PROGRAM APPROPRIATE?

You now have to determine whether there are problems in the areas of curriculum and instruction that result in referrals of students for evaluation for placement in special education and the eventual classification of students as LD. Charts 5.3A and 5.3B represent large and average size districts. In both districts, the lion's share of students referred for "academic" reasons came from the primary grades, and in both districts there were large numbers of students that came from grades K, 1, 2, and 3.

Chart 5.3A indicates that preschool to eleventh-grade students are referred for placement because of "academic" reasons. However, grades K−3 accounted for 61% of the referrals made for "academic"

CHART 5.2B **Intelligence Range of Students Referred and Transfer Students Who Were Eventually Classified LD by Gender.**

Intelligence Range	Column 1—Classified Learning Disabled		Column 2—Classified Transfers		Column 3—Not Classified Learning Disabled	
	Female	Male	Female	Male	Female	Male
Superior		1				2
High average	6	3				3
Average	7	11	2		2	5
Low average	4	4	2	5	2	1
Borderline	1	1	1	2		
Mentally deficient	1	1		1		
	19	21	5	8	4	11

CHART 5.3A Number of Times Terms Used by Grade for Initial Referrals (large district).

	Grade															
	PS	K	P1	1	2	3	4	5	6	7	8	9	10	11	12	Total
A. Academic Reasons	0	44	3	28	16	30	9	29	5	12	8	8	4	4	0	200

Terms used are those indicated in Chart 5.1.

CHART 5.3B Number of Times Terms Used by Grade (average size district).

	Grade														
	PS	K	1	2	3	4	5	6	7	8	9	10	11	12	Total
A. Academic Reasons	4	5	11	10	6	8	4	1	4	4	2	5	0	3	67

Terms used are those indicated in Chart 5.1.

CHART 5.4A Family Status of Students Referred for Evaluation (one district).

Initially Classified Learning Disabled		Classified Transfers	
Single Parent	Nuclear	Single Parent	Nuclear
22	53	37	30

CHART 5.4B Family Status of Students Referred for Evaluation (a second district).

Column 1—Classified Learning Disabled		Column 2— Classified Transfers		Column 3—Not Classified Learning Disabled	
Single Parent	Nuclear	Single Parent	Nuclear	Single Parent	Nuclear
12	28	5	8	4	11

reasons for initial referrals. Six students that eventually were classified LD were referred for evaluation for special education by their parents. Does Chart 5.3A provide you with sufficient information to warrant a closer look at the curriculum, instruction, expectations, and norms in grades K−3, 5, and 7? Does it provide you with sufficient information to inquire about the steps taken by classroom teachers to assist students with difficulties and problems?

Chart 5.3B indicates that preschool to twelfth-grade students were referred for placement because of "academic" reasons. However, three out of ten high school students were referred for failing classes. Does Chart 5.3B provide you with sufficient information to warrant a closer look at the curriculum, instruction, expectations, and norms in grades K−3, 4, and 10? Does it provide you with sufficient information to inquire about the steps taken by classroom teachers to assist students with difficulties and problems?

STEP 5 TO REDUCE THE SIZE OF THE STUDENT POOL

The fifth step that you need to take to ensure the equity, objectivity, and effectiveness of the referral process for students who are eventually classified LD is to make sure that students are not referred because the curriculum and instruction are developmentally inappropriate for the students. This means that you need to make sure that school psychologists know the curriculum, observe students as they function in class over a period of time, and analyze the appropriateness of teaching strategies, given students learning modalities. This is another way to reduce the pool of students referred for evaluation who do not need to be classified formally in order to receive the services they need.

REFERRALS BY STUDENT'S FAMILY STATUS

The purpose of this section is to determine whether students from single-parent households are more apt to be referred for evaluation for special education and eventually classified LD than one could reasonably expect from the general pool of students referred for special education. However, you may not have information about the family status of some students in your building or district.

In one district where 382 students were referred for special education, there was information available about the family composition of 369 families (97%). Of these 369 students, 217 (59%) were from a nuclear

family and 152 (33%) were from single-parent households.

Chart 5.4A indicates that 71% of referrals came from a nuclear household while 44% of transfer students came from nuclear households. However, 58% of LD students came from a nuclear family and 42% came from a single-parent household. Chart 5.4A will help you determine whether the services you provide are sufficient, need to be augmented, or need to be restructured. Do these students need academic help or do they need therapy? Will their academic performance improve if they receive emotional support?

In another district of the 106 students referred for special education, seventy-one (67%) were from a nuclear family and thirty-five (33%) were from single-parent households. Chart 5.4B (Columns 1 and 2) indicates that seventeen out of fifty-three (32%) students classified as LD came from single-parent households. This picture held true when one uses only in district students and excludes transfer students (Column 2). Columns 1 and 3 indicate that sixteen out of forty-eight (33%) students lived in a single-parent household.

STEP 6 TO REDUCE THE SIZE OF THE STUDENT POOL

The sixth step that you need to take to ensure the equity, objectivity, and effectiveness of the referral process for students who are eventually classified LD is to make sure that students from single-parent households are not referred because they are less empowered than their classmates. Also, you need to question whether classroom teachers are more apt to refer students from single-parent households for other than "academic" reasons. This is another way to reduce the pool of students referred for evaluation who do not need to be classified formally in order to receive the services they need.

SUMMARY

You now know how to audit the referral process of students who are eventually classified LD. You know what questions to ask the school psychologists when you find that many of the students referred and eventually classified LD are low-ability students who are referred for low achievement by the classroom teachers. You know to question the appropriateness of the academic program and the delivery of academic program when you find large numbers of students in primary grades referred for evaluation for special education and eventually classified LD. Finally, you know from my audits that approximately 35% of referred students that eventually are classified LD come from single-parent households. So if you find that your district refers and eventually classifies as LD a greater percent of students from single-parent households, raise questions. In essence, you have learned a quality assurance process. This helps you to ensure the equity, objectivity, and effectiveness of the referral process for students that are eventually classified LD. Also, this quality assurance process helps you to limit the growth of your LD program.

REFERENCES

Figueroa, R. A. (1991, September). ''The Reform of Assessment Practices in Special Education: The California Experience,'' lecture sponsored by the U.S. Office of Bilingual Education.

Gartner, A. and Lipsky, D. K. (1987). Beyond Special Education: Toward a Quality System for All Students, *Harvard Educational Review,* 57:367−395.

Ysseldyke, J. E., Algozzine, B., Shinn, M. and McGue, M. (1982). Similarities and Differences between Low Achievers and Students Labeled Learning Disabled. *Journal of Special Education,* 16:73−85.

6

Four Steps to Reduce the Number of Referrals of Students Eventually Classified Speech Impaired

AIM

THIS chapter gives you a detailed picture of the reasons for the large numbers of students referred for evaluation for placement in special education for "speech and language" difficulties. It helps you determine whether preschoolers and primary grade students are unnecessarily referred and classified SI, and it supplies you with information you need to determine whether services provided students are the most appropriate to help them remedy their speech and language difficulties. It explains four steps that you can take to slow down the SI classification as a growth industry. It focuses your attention on some of the doubts about these referrals, which may be made because of overly concerned parents and an overzealous speech and language department. There are illustrations and charts taken from audits that highlight points made about the referral process for students who eventually are classified SI. Snapshots of the referral process gathered by the method spelled out in this chapter help you develop more specific/meaningful SI criteria for the referral of students. You will be able to devise a customized quality control mechanism for your school/district. This helps you to better ensure that students who can be remediated at home and/or in class are not referred, that only those students who truly need services are referred, and that only students who need the services are classified SI, an important step to placing a lid on the proliferation of special education programs.

DEFINITION OF SPEECH IMPAIRED

The definition of a speech impaired youngster throughout the United States is basically similar to that of New York State. In New York State, the regulations of the New York commissioner of education defines speech impaired as "a pupil with a communication disorder, such as stuttering, impaired articulation, a language impairment or a voice impairment, which

adversely affects a child's educational performance." Please notice that there are not any operational definitions in this definition of SI. How does one define a language impairment? What is the operational definition of adversely?

JUSTIFICATIONS GIVEN FOR THE NUMBERS OF STUDENTS IDENTIFIED SPEECH IMPAIRED

I have implemented audits in districts where the percent of students classified SI exceeded the county average by 6.3% and the state average by 8.6%, yet in all the audits that I completed, I found, time after time, that classroom teachers, principals, psychologists, special education teachers, and members of the CSE justified the increased numbers of students identified SI. The reasons that they gave for the increased number of students identified SI covered a continuum. On one side of the continuum, there was the student's developmental process and on the other side of the continuum, there was the uniqueness of the special education and speech programs. Here is a list of reasons that you are apt to be given if there is an increase in the numbers of students identified as SI in your school/district:

- Students spent insufficient time in conversations at home and more time watching television and playing video games. These factors result in poor language development and the need to teach children to talk and listen to one another. There is a negative impact that speech handicaps have on reading, written language, and creative arts assignments.
- The acquisition of speech and language is directly related to a child's development. When there is a breakdown in this developmental process, it is readily noticed in the educational setting by comparison to others.
- Referred students have not developed receptive and expressive language skills, which are the basis for learning to read and write. With

proper and early intervention (preschool and primary grades), these problems can be remediated and usually are no longer seen at the secondary level.

- Most of the speech problems are related to language processing and some articulation problems.
- There are better screening methods by competent professionals that permit children to be identified earlier. This is essential because language is the basis for learning.
- The number of students classified SI is due to a successful early intervention program.
- This is due to parent referrals at preschool age and early identification through pre-K programs.
- Children with learning disabilities are being identified earlier than in the past, and most LDs are language-based and can benefit from related speech-language services.
- Speech problems are more easily recognizable by parents and others. This problem is open to remediation and responds to treatment.
- Speech problems respond to intervention and are very remediable.
- Because help is readily available, there are new referrals by parents and teachers each year.
- More people are aware of this service and bring their children in to be serviced sooner.
- There is an outstanding speech department that may be more capable of detecting students in need than departments in other districts.
- The speech department is seen very positively by the staff at large, and therefore there are more referrals made.
- The district is more methodical than other districts in classifying students for services.
- There is an excellent reputation of the special education program that draws parents to the district.

Notwithstanding these positive comments made to explain the size of the SI population, there are questions raised about the integrity of the process and program. These questions hint at steps you can take to reduce the number of students referred for speech and language reasons by your teachers and the number of students eventually classified SI.

DOUBTS RAISED ABOUT SPEECH AND LANGUAGE REFERRALS

Some classroom teachers, committee on special education (CSE) members, members of special educa-

tion departments, and principals in almost every district that I audited have questioned whether students needed to be classified SI and whether they were classified properly. Sample comments by some classroom teachers, CSE members, special education teachers, and principals in other districts probably mirror the thoughts of some of your own classroom teachers, CSE members, special education teachers, and principals. They have said:

- Speech and language services are not necessary all the time. What are they really doing? "Categories," "Categories," "Categories" every year!
- Speech impaired children in our district have to be classified to receive services, whereas in some other districts these children receive services without classification. We have accountability to consider.
- I don't feel unless there are other problems that speech is a reason for referral.
- There is perhaps a need for more established guidelines as to what conditions require service.
- Notwithstanding "rigorous guidelines" of the speech-language department and the fact that speech language deficits often coexist or exist prior to learning difficulties . . . a speech impaired label is quite often more palatable to a parent.
- Many parents have a problem labeling the child LD or EH and they settle for SI because it's less "severe" sounding.
- The increased number of students classified speech impaired was to defend the need for additional personnel in the special education department.
- Many SI students in other districts might be grouped into an LD category.
- Could it be easier to classify a student as SI rather than other classifications?
- This may be because SI is a less "damaging" label than others. If they qualify for SI, LD, or ED, a parent (teacher) may choose SI.
- A parent is more ready to accept an SI classification as opposed to an ED or LD.

STEP 1 TO REDUCE THE SIZE OF THE STUDENT POOL

The number of students referred for classification who eventually are classified SI in your district would be reduced if

- Parents of some of these students are instructed

on techniques and strategies to remediate their youngster's disability at home.
- Some students receive more thorough remediation in their classrooms.
- You make sure that children who were referred receive appropriate classifications, that is, that students who are not speech impaired should not be so classified.

REFERRALS BY GENDER

In order to analyze the equity, objectivity, and effectiveness of the referral process for students referred for evaluation for placement in special education who eventually are classified SI, you need to make use of the student database you created. The hard data tells you the number and percent of males and females that eventually are classified SI. The audits I conducted indicate that approximately 70% − 75% of referred students eventually classified as SI are males and 25% − 30% are females.

ILLUSTRATION: REFERRAL OF STUDENTS EVENTUALLY CLASSIFIED SI BY GENDER

With hard data generated by the database program, you can create a picture of the number of male and female students referred for special education who eventually are classified SI. I found that approximately 20% − 25% of referred students were eventually classified SI. Of the students eventually classified SI, from 70% − 75% were males and 25% − 30% were females. In one audit, eighty-nine (23%) of the 382 students referred for evaluation for placement for special education eventually were classified SI. Sixty-five students (73%) were males and twenty-four students (27%) were females.

The report that I wrote noted that:

236 of the 382 students referred for evaluation for special education placement were initial referrals and 146 students were transfer students. The initial referrals made up 30% of the 236 initial referrals who eventually were classified SI. Twelve percent of 146 transfers eventually were classified SI. In other words the number of students who came from the district rather than transfer students increased the percent of students who eventually were classified SI.

Seventy-three percent of the students referred for evaluation and eventually classified SI were males and 27% were females. The initial referrals had a higher percent of males (67% to 75%) and a lower percent of females (25% to 33%) eventually classified SI than the group of transfer students.

As a result of my findings from another audit, I wrote

Thirty-six students (34%) out of 106 students had been referred for evaluation for special education placement, at least partially, because district staff and/or parents were concerned about their speech. Twenty-four students (67%) were males and 12 students (33%) were females. Ultimately, 23 referred students (22%) were classified SI.

Eventually, of these thirty-six students, 23 (64%) were classified as SI, 8 were classified as LD, 3 (8%) were classified as Multi-Handicapped (MH) and 2 (5%) were not classified. Sixteen of the 23 students (70%) classified as SI were males and 7 students (30%) were females.

TERMS USED BY GENDER

In all the audits that I implemented, I never once came across "speech and language" comments made by classroom teachers in the referral process that had a districtwide standardized operational definition. This is especially surprising because, in many cases, there are more specific local criteria in place for the classification of students as SI than either LD or ED (emotionally handicapped). Notwithstanding this, the terms are a true representation of terms used by the teachers in your district who refer students who eventually are classified SI. It is recognized that these terms might be reorganized but any restructuring of these terms would not alter the findings.

STEP 2 TO REDUCE THE SIZE OF THE STUDENT POOL

It is clear that your school/district needs to develop standardized operational definitions of "speech and language" difficulties for classroom teachers who refer students for evaluations.

EXAMPLES OF TERMS AND PHRASES USED TO REFER STUDENTS

Charts 6.1A and 6.1B are good examples of the different level of detail that you can gather regarding the reasons given by classroom teachers for referrals of students who are eventually classified LD. Both charts indicate that boys in your school/district who are referred for evaluation for "speech and language" difficulties are likely to be referred for articulation problems.

Chart 6.1A is a good illustration of the different "speech and language" terms and phrases used to explain the reasons for the referral of students for

CHART 6.1A **Terms Related to Speech and Hearing Used to Refer Students for Placement in Special Education by Gender.**

	Terms Used	Males	Females
C.	Speech and hearing		
C.1	Speech and language deficits	8	1
C.2	Developmental speech delays	3	2
C.3	Articulation problems	14	1
C.4	Perceptual deficits	4	1
Totals		29	5

CHART 6.1B **More Detailed Terms Related to Speech and Hearing Used to Refer Students for Placement in Special Education by Gender.**

	Terms Used	Males	Females
C.	Speech and hearing		
C.1	Speech and language deficits	10	4
C.1.1	Speech and language needs identified		1
C.1.2	Deficits in the language processing areas	1	
C.1.3	Poor skills in following directions and language processing		1
C.1.4	Language processing	1	
	Subtotal speech and language deficits	12	6
C.2	Developmental speech delays		
C.2.1	Delayed language	1	
C.2.2	Gaps in development and acquisition of language/language based resource skills	1	1
C.2.3	Lag in speech development	1	
	Subtotal developmental speech delays	3	1
C.3	Articulation problems	3	
C.3.1	Unintelligible speech	1	
C.3.2	Severe articulation and syntactical problems	1	
	Subtotal articulation problems	5	0
C.4	Perceptual deficits		
C.4.1	Auditory/visual problems	1	
C.4.2	Auditory processing		1
	Subtotal perceptual deficits	1	1
C.5	Physical deficit		
C.5.1	Intermittent hearing loss	1	
C.5.2	Hearing loss/previously in special education		1
	Subtotal physical deficits	1	1
C.6	Memory	1	
C.6.1	Auditory memory		1
C.6.2	Word retrieval problem	1	
	Subtotal memory	2	1
C.7	Parent concern about speech	1	1
Totals		25	11

evaluation for placement in special education who eventually are classified SI. Chart 6.1A indicates the number of times each term or phrase is used for males and females. As you can see males who eventually are classified SI are frequently referred for articulation problems and speech and language deficits.

Chart 6.1B provides more details about the speech and language difficulties/problems that students experience according to classroom teachers in one district. Chart 6.1B indicates that, in one audit, females (55%) were more apt to be referred for speech and language deficit than males (48%) while males were more apt to be referred for articulation problems (20%) than females (0%).

STEP 3 TO REDUCE THE SIZE OF THE STUDENT POOL

The number of students referred for evaluation and eventually classified SI would be reduced if classroom teachers and speech therapists worked together in the classroom to service students that are mildly speech impaired. This is especially true for students who have speech and language deficits. However, you need to determine whether other children can be effectively remediated in the classroom given their age, the nature and severity of other impairments, and the number of students in the classroom.

NONSPEECH AND LANGUAGE REASONS GIVEN FOR STUDENTS THAT WERE EVENTUALLY CLASSIFIED SI

You need to remember, classroom teachers oftentimes give many different reasons for the referral of students. For instance, in one audit, 48% (forty-three) of students who were eventually classified SI also were referred for "academic" reasons. Six of the students who were eventually classified SI also were referred for "behavioral" reasons. Nine students who were eventually classified SI had been referred for evaluation for placement by their parents. In another audit in which thirty-six students had been referred for evaluation for "speech and language" problems twenty-three (64%) students eventually were classified as speech impaired, eight were classified as LD, three (8%) were classified as multi-handicapped and two (5%) were not classified.

Sixteen of the twenty-three students (70%) classified as speech impaired were males and seven students (30%) were females.

REFERRAL OF STUDENTS EVENTUALLY CLASSIFIED SI BY GRADE LEVEL

You will find that preschool/primary grade students make up the bulk of students referred for speech and language difficulties/problems. In my audits, I found that approximately 80% of the "speech and language" terms and phrases used by classroom teachers to refer students for evaluation for placement in special education related to students in grades PS to 1.

Chart 6.2A indicates that 80% (twenty-eight) of the "speech and language" terms used to refer students who eventually are classified SI occurred between grades PS and 1. Keep in mind that kindergarten students may have been referred for placement before they entered kindergarten.

Chart 6.2B gives you a more detailed breakdown of the "speech and language" terms and phrases used by classroom teachers in one audited district to refer students. Chart 6.2B indicates that all students who were referred for evaluation for special education for speech and hearing reasons were, with one exception, in preschool to third grade. You need to be aware of the fact that 50% of the terms used were for preschoolers. Preschoolers were the only students referred for developmental speech delays and articulation problems. With the exclusion of preschoolers, 67% of terms used for all other students referred for evaluation for special education cited speech and language deficits.

STEP 4 TO REDUCE THE SIZE OF THE STUDENT POOL

As an elementary school principal, you need to request a reevaluation of all PS students sent to you labeled SI. You will find that you can reduce the pool of kindergarten students referred for classification by merely reevaluating students just before school starts in August–September. This point was made by a kindergarten classroom teacher in one of the districts that I audited. She said, "The pre-K students should not be tested in the spring of the pre-K year—the children grow over the summer (give them time)."

CHART 6.2A Number of Times Terms Used by Grade.

		Grade															
		PS	K	P1	1	2	3	4	5	6	7	8	9	10	11	12	Total
C.	Speech and hearing	2	19	2	5	0	0	0	1	0	2	2	1	0	0	1	35

CHART 6.2B **Number of Times Terms Used by Grade (more detailed).**

Comments	Grade															Total
	PS	K	1	2	3	4	5	6	7	8	9	10	11	12	
C.1 Speech and language deficits	6	3	5	3	1										18
C.2 Developmental speech delays	4														4
C.3 Articulation problems	5														5
C.4 Perceptual deficits		1	1												2
C.5 Physical deficit					1					1					2
C.6 Memory	1		1	1											3
C.7 Parent concern about speech	2														2
Total	18	4	7	4	2	0	0	0	0	1	0	0	0	0	36

REFERRALS BY STUDENTS' INTELLIGENCE RANGE

Chart 6.3A indicates that 63% of the students for whom there was intelligence data available who were initial referrals that eventually were classified SI were in the average or above intelligence range. There were only eight transfer students for whom intelligence data was available. Six out of the eight students for whom intelligence data was available were in the average or above intelligence range. In the audits that I completed, I found that a greater percent of males with average and above intelligence range were referred for evaluation for speech and hearing reasons than females. This situation was more pronounced for students who were eventually classified speech impaired.

Chart 6.3B indicates that a greater percent of males in average and above intelligence range were referred for evaluation for speech and hearing reasons than females. This situation was more pronounced for students who were eventually classified speech impaired.

REFERRALS BY STUDENT'S FAMILY STATUS

The information gathered from my audits indicates that more of these students are apt to come from nuclear households than students referred for other reasons. Of the 382 students referred for special education, there was information available about the family composition of 369 families (97%). Of these 369 students, 217 (59%) were from a nuclear family and 152 (33%) were from single-parent households. Chart 6.4A indicates that 84% of initial referrals came from a nuclear household, while 64% of transfer students came from nuclear households. However, 80% of SI students came from a nuclear family and 20% came from a single-parent household.

In another audit, of the 106 students referred for special education, seventy-one (67%) were from a nuclear family and thirty-five (33%) were from single-parent households. Chart 6.4B indicates that 8% (three) of students referred for speech and hearing problems were from single-parent households. None of the twenty-three students classified speech impaired was from a single-parent household.

SUMMARY

You now know how to audit the referral process of students who are eventually classified SI. And you

CHART 6.3A **Intelligence Range of Students Referred for Speech and Hearing Reasons by Gender (one example).**

Intelligence Range	Initial Students Classified Speech Impaired		Transfer Students Classified Speech Impaired	
	Female	Male	Female	Male
High average		7		1
Average	4	20		5
Low average	5	10	1	
Borderline	3			
Mentally deficient				1
N/A	6	16	5	5
Totals	18	53	6	12

CHART 6.3B Intelligence Range of Students Referred for Speech and Hearing Reasons by Gender (a second example).

Intelligence Range	Students Classified Speech Impaired		Students *Not* Classified Speech Impaired	
	Female	Male	Female	Male
High average	2	2	1	
Average	2	12	1	5
Low average	2	2	3	
Borderline	1			
Mentally deficient				2
Totals	7	16	5	7

CHART 6.4A Referrals of Students by Family Status by Gender (one audit).

Initial Students Classified Speech Impaired		Transfer and Others Classified Speech Impaired	
Single-Parent House	Nuclear House	Single-Parent House	Nuclear House
11	59	6	11

CHART 6.4B Referrals of Students by Family Status by Gender (a second audit).

Students Classified Speech Impaired		Students *Not* Classified Speech Impaired	
Single-Parent House	Nuclear House	Single-Parent House	Nuclear House
0	23	3	10

know the specific areas to check if you want to reduce the number of students referred for evaluation for placement in special education because of "speech and language" difficulties. You know to question whether all the preschoolers that have been classified need to be classified. Will some of these youngsters "outgrow" their difficulties by the time they enter kindergarten? Could some of these youngsters be remediated at home by their parents? Could some of these youngsters be helped in their classrooms by the classroom teachers? Could some of these youngsters be remediated in their classroom by speech therapists? And could some of these youngsters only be treated in a self-contained setting because of the number of students in their classroom and the severity of their speech difficulties? You know to question whether some of the "speech and language" difficulties could be treated in the classroom, especially speech and language deficits. And you know that you could reduce the number of students classified SI merely by making sure that only children who were truly SI received an SI classification. In essence, you have learned a quality assurance process. This helps you to ensure the equity, objectivity, and effectiveness of the referral process for students that are eventually classified SI. Also, this quality assurance process helps you to limit the growth of your SI program.

7

Six Steps to Reduce the Number of Referrals of Students Eventually Classified Emotionally Disturbed

AIM

THIS chapter shows you six steps to take to reduce the number of students referred for evaluation for placement in special education, who eventually are classified ED. There are charts and examples to help you see how variables such as the student's gender, terms and phrases used by classroom teachers, student's grade level, the family status of students, and the socioeconomic status of students influence the referral of students who eventually are classified ED. You will come to grip with the question of whether socioeconomic forces and gender differences pervert the intention of special education and undermine the integrity of the ED classification. There are a series of questions you will be able to answer factually that have an impact on the referral process and the size of the ED population in your school/district:

- Is special education the only alternative that classroom teachers have to rid themselves of some demanding/bothersome students?
- Are some students referred because they fail to live up to norms and expectations set by classroom teachers and not because they are emotionally handicapped?
- Does the clash over norms and expectations reflect, at times, socioeconomic and gender differences between some students and some classroom teachers?
- Are less affluent students more apt to be referred and eventually classified ED?
- Does the referral and eventual classification of students as ED reflect the lack of empowerment of some single-parent students?

Snapshots of the referral process gathered by the method spelled out in this chapter help you develop more specific/meaningful ED criteria for the referral of students. You will be able to devise a customized quality control mechanism for your school/district to better ensure that only those students who truly need services are referred. That is a first step to placing a lid on the proliferation of special education programs.

REFERRALS OF STUDENTS WHO WERE EVENTUALLY CLASSIFIED EMOTIONALLY DISTURBED

Although it might surprise you that approximately 15% of students referred for evaluation eventually are classified ED, it might cause you to question the appropriateness of this classification once you have a series of pictures of referred students who eventually are classified ED. You can determine whether these referrals are appropriate or inappropriate. If inappropriate, you will be able to determine if there is either gender, racial/ethnic, and/or socioeconomic bias in the referral and classification of students or a district/school mentality that encourages the referral and classification of demanding/bothersome students.

You know that there are some demanding/bothersome students in your school, and you know that even one student in a regular classroom can disrupt the teaching and learning that takes place in that classroom. No one doubts that your demanding/bothersome students are pains in the necks of teachers and other students. What you do not know is whether each and every one of these demanding/bothersome students is ED. You do not know whether some of these students are thought to be demanding/bothersome because they clash with the norms/expectations set by classroom teachers or because they are ED. You do not know whether the norms/expectations set by classroom teachers are appropriate given the age, gender, and socioeconomic status of students, and you do not know whether some of these students are demanding/bothersome because the program delivered is not challenging enough for them. Furthermore, you do not know whether some of these demanding/bothersome students are referred for evaluation for placement in special education because classroom teachers are not given other alternatives to help themselves, their other students, and the demanding/bothersome students. However, your job is to make sure that students who are referred and eventually classified really are ED.

DEFINITION OF EMOTIONALLY DISTURBED

In the audits that I implemented, I found that approximately 15% of students grades K – 12 referred for special education are eventually classified ED. The definition of an emotionally disturbed youngster throughout the United States is basically similar to that of New York State. In New York State, the regulations of the New York commissioner of education defines emotionally disturbed as

> A pupil with an inability to learn which cannot be explained by intellectual, sensory or health factors and who exhibits one or more of the following characteristics over a long period of time and to a marked degree:
>
> (i) an inability to build or maintain satisfactory interpersonal relationships with peers and teachers;
>
> (ii) inappropriate types of behavior or feelings under normal circumstances;
>
> (iii) a generally pervasive mood of unhappiness or depression; or
>
> (iv) a tendency to develop physical symptoms or fears associated with personal or school problems.
>
> The term does not include socially maladjusted pupils unless it is determined that they are emotionally disturbed.

Please notice that there are not any operational definitions in this definition of ED. How does one define a "marked degree"? How subjective are the phrases "satisfactory interpersonal relationships," "inappropriate types of behavior or feelings," "a generally pervasive mood of unhappiness," and "a tendency to develop symptoms"?

STEP 1 TO REDUCE THE SIZE OF THE STUDENT POOL

You can reduce the number of children referred for "behavioral" reasons if you provide classroom teachers with a better definition of the standards/criteria for classification of an ED student. It is clear that your school/district needs to develop standardized operational definitions of "behavioral" difficulties for classroom teachers who refer students for evaluations.

REFERRALS BY GENDER

In order to analyze the equity, objectivity, and effectiveness of the referral process for students referred for evaluation for placement in special education who eventually are classified ED, you need to make use of the student database you created. The hard data tells you the number and percent of males and females that eventually are classified ED.

ILLUSTRATION: REFERRAL OF STUDENTS EVENTUALLY CLASSIFIED ED BY GENDER

With hard data generated by the database program, you can create a picture of the number of male and female students referred for special education who eventually are classified ED. I found that approximately 15% of referred students were eventually classified ED. Of the students eventually classified ED, between 59% and 73% were males and between 27% and 41% were females. In one audit, fifty-nine (15%) of the 382 students referred for evaluation for placement for special education eventually were classified ED. Thirty-five students (59%) were males and twenty-four students (41%) were females. I have found that districts are less likely to classify students ED when they are referred for evaluation from within the district. They are more likely to classify students ED when they transfer into their districts.

The report that I wrote noted that

> Fifty-nine (15%) of the 382 students referred for evaluation for special education placement were eventually classified Emotionally Handicapped. Thirty-five (59%) were males and 24 (41%) were females.

> It is important to note that 236 of the 382 students referred for evaluation for special education placement were initial referrals and 146 students were transfer students (139). The initial referrals made up 11% of the 236 initial referrals who were eventually classified ED. The transfer students made up 23% of 146 transfer students. In other words the transfer students increased the percent of students who were eventually classified ED.

> Fifty-nine percent of the students referred for evaluation and eventually classified ED were males and 41% were females. The transfer students had a higher percent of females (45% to 35%) and lower percent of males (55% to 65%) eventually classified ED than the group of students that were initial referrals.

In another audit, I wrote:

> Fifteen students (14%) of the 106 students referred for evaluation for special education placement were eventually classified Emotionally Disturbed. Eleven (73%) were males and 4 (27%) were females.

It is important to note that 22 students had been referred for evaluation for special education placement, at least partially, because district staff and/or parents were concerned about their poor/inappropriate behavior. Eighteen of the 22 students (82%) were males and 4 students (18%) were females.

Eventually, of these 22 students, 12 (55%) were classified as Emotionally Disturbed, 5 (23%) were classified as Learning Disabled, 2 (9%) were classified as Speech Impaired, 3 (33%) were not classified. Eighteen of the 22 students (67%) classified as Emotionally Disturbed were males and 4 students (33%) were females.

Three other students were eventually classified Emotionally disturbed. These 3 male students were new entrants who had been in special education programs.

STEP 2 TO REDUCE THE SIZE OF THE STUDENT POOL

You can reduce the size of the student pool if you can educate classroom teachers to distinguish between demanding/bothersome students and emotionally handicapped students. You need to determine the reasons that so many males are referred for "behavioral" reasons. You need to be sure that classroom norms/expectations that males have violated are age and gender appropriate. Also, you need to reevaluate the ED classification of transfer students, especially males. This does not mean that all transfer students will be declassified. What it does mean is that, in some instances, there may be individual students that will not qualify under your spelled out criteria.

TERMS USED TO REFER STUDENTS

In all the audits that I implemented, I never once came across "behavioral" comments made by classroom teachers in the referral process that had a districtwide

standardized operational definition. Notwithstanding this, the terms are a true representation of terms used by the teachers in your district who refer students who eventually are classified ED. It is recognized that these terms might be reorganized but any restructuring of these terms would not alter the findings.

EXAMPLES OF TERMS AND PHRASES USED TO REFER STUDENTS

Charts 7.1A and 7.1B are good examples of the different levels of detail that you can gather regarding the reasons given by classroom teachers for referrals of students who are eventually classified ED. Both charts indicate that boys in your school/district who are referred for evaluation for "behavioral" difficulties are likely to be referred for "inappropriate socialization skills." Girls are more likely than boys to be referred for "maladjustment" difficulties.

Chart 7.1A is a good illustration of the different "behavioral" terms and phrases used to explain the reasons for the referral of students for evaluation for placement in special education who eventually are classified ED. Although there is not a sufficient number of terms used for students who were eventually classified ED to make any generalization for all districts, Chart 7.1A points out that the term/phrase used for males who were eventually classified ED was "inappropriate socialization skills." However, 22% (13) of fifty-nine students who were eventually classified ED also were referred for "academic" reasons. Four of the students who were eventually classified ED also were referred for "speech and language" reasons. Three students who were eventually classified ED had been referred for evaluation for placement by their parents.

Chart 7.1B indicates that females were more apt to be referred for "attention deficit disorders" (42%) and "maladjustment difficulties" (25%), while males were more apt to be referred for "inappropriate socialization skills" (37%).

CHART 7.1A Terms Related to Academic Performance Used to Refer Students for Placement in Special Education by Gender.

	Terms Used	Males	Females
B.	Behavior		
B.1	Attention deficit disorders	1	0
B.2	Behavior adjustment difficulties	1	2
B.3	Inappropriate socialization skills	3	1
B.4	Maladjustment difficulties	1	2
B.5	Hospitalized	1	1
Total		7	6

CHART 7.1B More Detailed Terms Related to Academic Performance Used to Refer Students for Placement in Special Education by Gender.

	Terms Used	Males	Females
B.	Behavior		
B.1	Attention deficit disorders	1	1
B.1.1	Attention deficits		1
B.1.2	Attention deficit qualities	1	
B.1.3	Attention difficulties affect other subjects	3	2
B.1.4	Preoccupied and unable to attend to the task at hand		1
Subtotal		5	5
B.2	Behavioral adjustment difficulties		1
B.2.1	Emotional behavioral factors	1	
B.2.2	Inappropriate behavior		1
B.2.3	Extremely impulsive	1	
B.2.4	Number of suspensions due to conflict	1	
B.2.5	Oppositional disorder	1	
B.2.6	Highly frustrated	1	
Subtotal		5	2
B.3	Inappropriate socialization skills		
B.3.1	Fire setting in school	1	
B.3.2	Difficulties relating to peers, adults, others	6	2
B.3.3	Difficulties participating in a group of only twelve children	1	
B.3.4	Chooses to play alone or with one or at most two other children	1	
B.3.5	Poor school sdjustment	1	
Subtotal		10	2
B.4	Maladjustment difficulties		
B.4.1	Attendance		2
B.4.2	Fights not to come into the classroom	1	
B.4.3	Lack of maturity		1
B.4.4	Dysthemia	1	
B.4.5	A great deal of time fantasizing	1	
Subtotal		3	3
B.5	Hospitalized	1	
B.6	Classified ED in previous district	3	
Total		27	12

CHART 7.2A Number of Times Terms Used by Grade.

							Grade									
	PS	K	P1	1	2	3	4	5	6	7	8	9	10	11	12	Total
B. Behavior	0	1	0	1	1	0	1	1	1	1	2	1	0	3	0	13

STEP 3 TO REDUCE THE SIZE OF THE STUDENT POOL

You can reduce the number of students referred, especially males, by developing an operational definition of "inappropriate socialization skills." You need to make sure that the socialization expectations and norms set by classroom teachers are appropriate for the age, gender, and socioeconomic background of students.

REFERRAL OF STUDENTS BY GRADE LEVEL

You need to know that middle school and high school students are more likely than elementary students to be referred for evaluation for placement in special education and eventually classified ED. You can see this in both Charts 7.2A and 7.2B.

Chart 7.2A indicates that there were too few terms used for students who were eventually classified ED to make any generalizations for all students in all schools/districts. However, it is interesting to note that behavior problems among initial referrals was greater for secondary students than for elementary students in the district and that this phenomenon exists in other schools/districts that I audited.

Chart 7.2B indicates that 48% of the comments concerned preschoolers to fourth grades, 31% of the comments concerned fifth to eighth graders, and 18% of comments concerned high school students. Notice that preschoolers and kindergartners are referred for "attention deficit disorders," "behavior adjustment difficulties," "inappropriate socialization skills," and "maladjustment difficulties." Middle school students are referred primarily for "inappropriate socialization skills" and "maladjustment difficulties." High school students are referred mainly for "inappropriate socialization skills."

STEP 4 TO REDUCE THE SIZE OF THE STUDENT POOL

You can reduce the size of the student pool if you can reduce the number of secondary students referred for "behavioral" reasons. You need to be sure that some of these referrals are not due to the "menacing" size of male students who fail to conform to classroom norms/expectations nor a distorted male view of "independence" nor a clash of wills.

REFERRALS BY STUDENTS' INTELLIGENCE RANGE

You might be interested in the fact that my audits indicate that a greater percent of students referred for evaluation for placement in special education who eventually are classified ED are in the average or above average intelligence range than students who are eventually classified LD and SI.

Chart 7.3A indicates that 71% of the students for whom there was intelligence data available who were initial referrals that were eventually classified ED were in the average or above average intelligence range. There were sixteen transfer students for whom intelligence data was available. Eight out of the sixteen (50%) students for whom intelligence data was avail-

CHART 7.2B Number of Times Terms Used by Grade (more detailed).

Comments	Grade														Total
	PS	K	1	2	3	4	5	6	7	8	9	10	11	12	
B.1 Attention deficit disorders	3	1	1	0	2	1	0	1	0	1	0	0	0	0	10
B.2 Behavioral adjustment difficulties	0	2	0	1	1	0	0	1	0	0	1	1	0	0	7
B.3 Inappropriate socialization skills	2	1	0	0	0	1	2	0	2	0	0	3	0	1	12
B.4 Maladjustment difficulties	2	0	0	0	0	0	0	1	1	1	0	1	0	0	6
B.5 Hospitalized	0	0	0	0	0	0	1	0	0	0	0	0	0	0	1
B.6 Classified ED in previous district	0	0	0	0	0	1	1	1	0	0	0	0	0	0	3
Total	7	4	1	1	3	3	4	4	3	2	1	5	0	1	39

CHART 7.3A Intelligence Range of Students Referred for Behavioral Reasons by Gender (one audit).

Intelligence Range	Initially Classified ED		Transfer Classified ED	
	Female	Male	Female	Male
Superior				
High average	2	1	1	
Average	2	5	2	5
Low average	1	1		6
Borderline	1	1	1	
Mentally deficient			1	
N/A	3	9	10	7
Total	9	17	15	18

CHART 7.3B Intelligence Range of Students Referred for Behavioral Reasons by Gender (a second audit).

Intelligence Range	Initially Classified ED		Transfer Classified ED		Not Classified ED	
	Female	Male	Female	Male	Female	Male
Superior		1				1
High average	1	4			1	
Average	2	3		3	2	4
Low average	1				1	1
Borderline						
Mentally deficient						
Total	4	8	0	3	4	6

CHART 7.4A Family Status of Students Referred for Evaluation (one example).

Initially Classified ED		Transfer Classified ED	
Single Parent	Nuclear	Single Parent	Nuclear
16	8	31	2

CHART 7.4B Family Status of Students Referred for Evaluation (a second example).

Initially Classified ED		Transfer Classified ED		Not Classified ED	
Single Parent	Nuclear	Single Parent	Nuclear	Single Parent	Nuclear
5	7	3	0	2	8

able were in the average or above average intelligence range. These data indicate that 64% of females and 58% of males who were eventually classified ED for whom intelligence data was available were in the average and above average intelligence ranges.

Chart 7.3B indicates that sixteen out of seventeen (94%) males and six out of eight (75%) females referred for "behavioral" reasons were in the average and above average intelligence ranges. Three students referred for evaluation for placement in special education for "behavioral" reasons were not classified at all. All three students were males. One student was in the superior and two were in the average intelligence ranges. Five students were eventually classified LD. Two students were eventually classified SI.

STEP 5 TO REDUCE THE SIZE OF THE STUDENT POOL

You can reduce the size of the student pool if you can reduce the number of students referred for "behavioral" reasons because they found the academic work to be either too difficult or too easy. In other words, "academic" problems triggered "behavioral" problems.

REFERRALS BY STUDENTS' FAMILY STATUS

Through my audits, I have found that there is a substantial range (40%–67%) in the percent of students referred and eventually classified ED who come from single-parent/foster families. However, this percentage exceeds that of students referred and eventually classified LD or SI. Furthermore, in one audit, I found that 25% of students referred and eventually classified ED received free or reduced lunch in school. This was slightly greater than students eventually classified LD (23%) and much greater than students eventually classified SI (16%).

Chart 7.4A indicates that 67% of students who were initial referrals and 94% of transfer students who were eventually classified ED lived in a single-parent household.

Chart 7.4B indicates that 40% (ten out of twenty-five) of students referred for behavioral reasons lived in a single-parent household. However, that figure decreases when one considers only those students referred from within district.

STEP 6 TO REDUCE THE SIZE OF THE STUDENT POOL

You can reduce the pool of students by providing remedial support services, such as guidance and counseling, for male secondary students from single-parent households whose actions clash with the norms and expectations set by classroom teachers. These students tend to be slightly less affluent than students referred and eventually classified LD and substantially less affluent than students referred and eventually classified SI.

SUMMARY

You now know how to audit the referral process of students who are eventually classified ED. And you know that you need to make sure that referrals are truly justified based upon well-defined operational terms and criteria. You need to be sure that the referrals are not the attempt of classroom teachers to rid themselves of some demanding/bothersome students who are not emotionally handicapped. You are able to determine whether some students are referred because they fail to live up to norms and expectations set by classroom teachers and not because they are emotionally handicapped. You know the signs that indicate that clashes over norms and expectations reflect, at times, socioeconomic and gender differences between some students and some classroom teachers. You are sensitive to the fact that, at times, less affluent students are referred and eventually classified ED. And you know that the lack of empowerment of some single-parent households results in the referral and classification of students as ED. You know that you could reduce the number of students classified ED merely by making sure that only children who were truly ED received an ED classification. In essence, you have learned a quality assurance process. This helps you to ensure the equity, objectivity, and effectiveness of the referral process for students that are eventually classified ED. Also, this quality assurance process helps you to limit the growth of your ED program.

8

The Committee on Special Education

AIM

THIS chapter provides you with a series of snapshots of the committee on special education and identifies five steps that you can take to make the CSE a more equitable, objective, and effective "gatekeeper." There are charts and examples to help you see how such variables as a student's race/ethnicity and gender influence the CSE and the classification process. The chapter explains the membership of the CSE. You will be able to see how the CSE functions. The tasks that fall to the chairperson of the CSE are identified. You will learn of the pivotal role of school psychologists and the subtleties that surround their assessment of students. Also, you will be able to note the limited role of building principals in the CSEs. Finally, the chapter spells out five steps to take to make sure that the CSE functions in a responsible and equitable manner. These five steps help you to downsize the number of students classified by your CSE.

OVERVIEW OF CONCERNS

In order to ensure the equity, objectivity, and effectiveness of the classification process, you need to be sure that the CSE functions properly. The CSE has the legal responsibility in your district to determine the appropriate placement for students referred for special education. This makes it a "gatekeeper." Right now the term *effective gatekeeper* is an oxymoron much like "meaningful faculty meeting," "military intelligence," and "intelligent and sensitive news broadcasters." What else can you conclude? You know that, in all likelihood, your district does not have well-defined standards and criteria in place to determine whether a student is LD or ED. You know that the terms used to define LD and ED are vague and nebulous, yet approximately 60% of classified students fall into one of these two categories. This means that a student

judged to be handicapped by one CSE in one district may not be classified by another district. Moreover, if there are two or more CSEs in your district, it is possible that a student classified by one of the CSEs would not be classified by the others. You know that the integrity of school psychologists is suspect, yet they are, at the very least, one among equals and more likely the central force on the CSE. You are better able to downsize the special education program and reduce costs if you can make the CSE a more effective "gatekeeper." To do this, you need to know the manner in which it functions and the perceptions that CSE members have of the decision-making process.

COMPOSITION OF THE COMMITTEE OF SPECIAL EDUCATION

As you know, the committee of special education is the group that decides whether a referred student is to be classified. The membership of the CSE is legally spelled out for you. In New York, Education Law 4402 (1B1) and Part 200.4 (C3) of the regulations of the commissioner of education spell out the membership of the committee of special education. The members include a school psychologist, a representative of the school district, a physician, a parent member, the child's classroom teacher, the parent of the child, and anyone else designated by the board of education.

NUMBER OF CSEs

As a result of my audits, I now know that the number of CSEs in a district may vary according to the number of students in the district. In most cases, there is only one CSE in a district; however, I audited a district that had 15,000 students and sixteen separate CSEs. In such districts, there are logistical problems to work out just in terms of assignments of members of the CSE. In one large district, CSEs were staffed from a pool of approximately seventy to eighty people. There was a major CSE and building CSEs. The members of building CSEs were rotated and selected from personnel from other buildings in the district. Each and every building CSE was chaired by a psychologist or by the assistant superintendent for pupil personnel services and special education. It was estimated that there was a CSE meeting at least five times a month from September to February and more often than that from March to June.

You might be interested in the fact that, as a result of my recommendations, the director of special education restructured the CSEs. Rather than sixteen, there are now four CSEs. Rather than the CSEs meeting in each building, each of the four CSEs meet in the district office, monitored by the director of special education, and rather than blanket approval of any test requested by parents, the director of special education only approves tests that will yield information about a student's performance in school. The director of special education has stopped a widespread practice in the district of testing students because parents want information about their youngsters.

STEP 1 TO REDUCE THE SIZE OF THE STUDENT POOL

The first step that you can take to ensure equity, objectivity, and effectiveness of the CSE is to monitor the operation of the CSE closely and regularly. In addition, the fewer the number of CSEs, the more likely you are to have a more consistent classification process.

ATTENDANCE AT CSE MEETINGS

You need to be aware of the fact that members of the CSE may attend up to forty CSE meetings a year, especially in large districts. In audit after audit, when I asked members of the CSE to indicate the different people that were present at these meetings the most optimistic account of those in attendance, in descending order, were

- chairperson (100%)
- psychologists (100%)
- speech language therapists (100%)
- educational evaluator (100%)
- social worker (100%)
- regular education teacher (100%)
- special education teachers/resource room teachers (100%)
- parents of student (95 %)
- parent member of CSE (93%)
- building administrator (85%)

PRINCIPALS

In most of the audits, I found that principals attended 20% to 60% of CSE meetings. According to principals in one district, each principal attended CSE meetings between 20% and 50% of the time. The middle school principal noted that he attended whenever he anticipated difficulties with parents and when he disagreed with the recommendations of the psychologist. The high school principal noted that a high school administrator was present 90% of the time that these meetings concerned high school students. Also, he attended whenever he thought it was warranted and when he was requested to serve on the committee as the administrator. In another district, the seven principals attended an average of 57% of CSE meetings. The three assistant principals attended an average of 97% of CSE meetings (Weinstein, 1989). This indicates that pupil personnel and special education staff have more influence and control over CSE and the classification process than building principals.

STEP 2 TO REDUCE THE SIZE OF THE STUDENT POOL

In effective schools, building administrators take responsibility for program effectiveness. If building administrators are to play a similar role in promoting effective special education programs, they need to know the guidelines and develop measurable criteria for classification of students. And they need to attend CSE meetings. If you want to reduce costs and downsize the special education program, then you have to be a knowledgeable participant at CSE meetings.

THE CLASSIFICATION PROCESS

The classification process for student placement in special education follows the same steps from district to district according to my audits. The CSE receives reports and recommendations from the psychologist, classroom teacher, education evaluator, social worker, parent, and others about the student. The CSE receives information about the student's performance in class, grades, behavior, IQ, other testing results, informal observations, and input from parents and school personnel. The CSE members listen to each presenter's reports, question unclear information, discuss the information, weigh the reports and recommendations, and reach a consensus. According to some chairpersons of CSEs, the committee spends approximately forty-five minutes deliberating about each child. However, some CSE members have raised questions about the effectiveness and efficiency of the process. In one audit, one CSE member cautioned, "In my building, there is an antiquated, cumbersome process to even get a referral. Once that is accomplished, the process to finally achieve service can take longer than a year."

ROLE OF THE PSYCHOLOGISTS

You need to be aware that the perception of the role of the psychologist varies from one among equals to the key person on the CSE according to some CSE members, principals, and psychologists. Some of your CSE members, principals, and psychologists are apt to paint the psychologist as one member of a team and state:

- The psychologist is a member of the team; we all have equal input to the process.
- We function as a team. We jointly decide on the classification of a child. The psychologist provides insight and IQ scores for the team to consider when deciding on a classification.
- The psychologist is part of the multidisciplinary team. Each member contributes an assessment of the child based on formal and informal data collection.
- There is nothing unique about the role of sitting psychologist. He/she is another professional with a particular perspective who must work collectively to understand the parameters from which a student is referred.
- I am one committee member and assist in interpretation of data presented, make recommendations, and help prepare the IEP for a student.
- The psychologist is a consultant at every step. He/she is no more "powerful" than anyone else at the CSE.
- The psychologist collects all data, makes the initial recommendation, and is a presenting spokesperson but is one among equals on the CSE.

However, other CSE members are apt to describe the tasks of the psychologists and give you an insight into his/her importance. They are apt to tell you that

- The psychologist does testing, the social worker provides a family history, the speech/language therapist does a workup of language skills, the medical doctor reports any physical handicap, and the classroom teacher reports on student learning.
- She/he gathered background material, interpreted, and explained the information to the committee.

- The tasks that psychologists have that make them important members of teams included analysis, testing, and diagnosis. Also, they are concerned about the placement of students and the parents and teachers they deal with and encounter.
- The psychologist evaluates the cognitive/emotional aspects of the student. The special educator evaluates learning disability issues and the speech/language therapist evaluates issues relating to speech and language development.
- The psychologist completes a standardized test battery, which helps determine the existence of a handicapping condition by providing an intelligence quotient and projectives.
- The psychologist will do testing on the child to determine the child's aptitude and to recognize any other problems as far as home environment, school setting, or psychological factors that must be taken into account in order to evaluate.

Finally, other CSE members are apt to spell out the key role that psychologists play in the classification process. In one district, nine out of ten school administrators regarded the school psychologists as most significant in the decision-making process. Here are samples of comments your CSE members might make

- The psychologist certainly has a major contributing role with regard to assessment.
- The referral is made by a parent and/or guidance counselor to the CSE chairperson via the psychologist who then tests the child, after which other selected staff test. The psychologist presents findings to staff and to CSE. He has the authority in the building.
- The psychologist tries to head up the team. He acts as the liaison to PPS.
- The psychologist has an essential role — especially for children with emotional handicapping conditions.
- I feel the psychologists' input plays a crucial role in the classification process. They supply important information about the child that may affect the recommendations.
- Psychologists are important in decisions related to learning disabled and emotionally disturbed classifications. The psychologist has a pivotal role in the CSE.
- The psychologist have the most important role on the CSE. This is due to the fact that the psychologist interpreted test data used in decision making.

WEIGHT OF ASSESSMENT

The Importance of Classroom Teacher Comments

You get an inkling about the importance of the teachers from the comments made by psychologists and principals about the weight given to classroom teacher comments and assessment data in the classification of students. In one audit, both psychologists and principals placed equal weight on classroom teachers' comments and assessment data in decision making regarding the classification of students. The comments of those who thought teacher statements and assessment data were of equal importance were summed up by one psychologist who wrote that both were an ''integral part of a comprehensive evaluation of a student.''

You find that some principals indicate that they placed at least the same weight on assessment data and teacher comments. Psychologists point out that test data are used in conjunction with observations and parent/teacher information to adequately assess a child. Principals and psychologists stress that no one assessment device is used to form a decision on classification. They tell you that the ''teacher's report and participation at the CSE is very important. The firsthand resource of the professional working with the child daily is very valuable.'' You find that they use terms such as ''extremely relevant,'' ''crucial,'' ''very relevant,'' ''very important,'' ''extremely important,'' and ''imperative'' to characterize classroom teacher statements.

The Importance of Assessment Data

In my audits, I found that there were principals and psychologists who thought that assessment data was more important than information supplied by teachers. In one district, principals pointed out that all information was assessed and evaluated. The strongest statement made regarding assessment data was that ''it was very important in determining if the child is eligible for services and should be classified.'' In another district, all principals indicated that they placed greater weight on assessment data than they did on teacher comments, even those who viewed teacher comments as important information for members of the CSE to have when reaching decisions about the placement of students in special education. They were concerned that some classroom teachers had inappropriate expectations for students. Some teachers had emotional reactions to students. One principal regretted that students had been classified inappropriately based on teacher statements. On the other hand, you have psychologists note that the assessment devices they use are ''chosen because of their strong psychometric measurement including validity and reliability.'' They regard assessment data as highly significant because ''it provides the diagnostic evidence for classification. These objective measures use normative samples with high reliability and validity coefficients.''

REPORTS AND RESEARCH REGARDING ASSESSMENT

Gender Bias

You need to be aware of the concerns that exist regarding tests administered in your school/district even if your school/district is Lilly white. First, you get an idea of the need for vigilance in an article entitled ''The Role of Sex Differences in the Referral Process as Measured by the Peabody Picture Vocabulary Test—Revised and the Wechsler Intelligence Scale for Children—Revised'' (*Psychology in the Schools,* 1989). The report indicates the gender bias of the PPVT-R and WISC-R. And even though these particular tests may not be used by your school/district, it points out the need to be careful in the selection of tests. As a matter of fact, I found in a recent audit that sixteen psychologists indicated that the assessment devices used most frequently, in descending order, were

- Connor Rating Scales (12)
- Bender-Gestalt (10)
- Stanford Binet (10)
- BASIS Achievement Test (8)
- Berry Developmental Test of Visual-Motor Inventory (7)
- ACTES (7)
- WISC III (6)
- TAT (6)

You might be interested in the effect of this information on the psychologists, speech therapists, and special education teachers. First, they pointed out that the PPVT-R is strictly used as a receptive vocabulary test for one-word vocabulary and not as an IQ test. It is used in conjunction with an expressive one-word test to document any discrepancy in this area. Second, they pointed out that many speech therapists do not utilize this test for receptive vocabulary any longer due to particular biases that it may exhibit due to the outdated nature of the revised material. They pointed out that, in place of the PPVT-R, they use

- Comprehensive Receptive Expressive Vocabulary Test (CREVT)
- Receptive One Word Vocabulary Test (ROWVT)
- Woodcock Language Proficiency Battery (WLPB)

- Test of Language Development (TOLD)
- Comprehensive Evaluation of Language Function (CELF-R)

Racial/Ethnic Bias

You need to know that the *Larry P.* settlement (1986) in California was a landmark decision concerning IQ tests and African American students. The settlement

> prohibits the use of IQ tests with Black pupils for special education purposes. IQ tests are construed to mean any test which purports to be or is understood to be a standardized test of intelligence. . . . In making a determination of whether a test falls under the IQ test ban for Black pupils one should consider:
>
> Is the test standardized and does it purport to measure intelligence (cognitive, mental ability or aptitude)?
>
> Are the test results reported in the form of IQ or mental age?
>
> Does evidence of the (construct) validity of the test rely on correlations with IQ tests?
>
> An affirmative answer to any of the above indicates that use of the test may fall within the ban. (*Larry P. v. Riles,* 495 F. Supp. 926 (1979), p. 931; Larry P. Task Force Report, 1989).

The net effect of this information should make you skeptical of placing reliance on tests administered by psychologists.

STEP 3 TO REDUCE THE SIZE OF THE STUDENT POOL

You can reduce the number of referred students classified if you monitor the actions of the psychologists and make psychologists accountable by raising questions when you have doubts about their statements or judgments. Are students only given tests that are essential? Are the judgments made by psychologists based upon factual knowledge of curriculum, direct observation of classroom instruction, and unbiased data? Do psychologists have a disproportionate role in the CSE? Does the building administrator rubber stamp all recommendations made by psychologists?

ROLE OF THE SPECIAL EDUCATION DIRECTOR

In each of the districts that I audited, the assistant superintendent for pupil personnel and special education/or the director of special education served, at times, as chair of the CSE and played key roles in CSE meetings. In a number of instances, CSE members questioned the administrator's role at CSE meetings. You are likely to hear some CSE members complain that

the administrator of the program is not usually at the meetings or that the administrator provides very little technical guidance. However, you can form a job description for a chair of your CSE from comments made by CSE members regarding the tasks of the chair. Here are some of the tasks identified:

- records all the information and results of the meeting; guides the meetings and has an unending amount of knowledge with regard to special education
- attends controversial meetings and serves as a resource in difficult cases; make sure that recommendations and directives from the committee were implemented
- chairs meetings; guides meetings to a successful decision
- is instrumental in the placement and provision of services for all CSE students – oversees all
- oversees difficult cases, an advocate for the child and his/her parents
- oversees the programs that are implemented and makes sure children are placed in the best setting possible
- chairs committee but also act as resource person
- chairs the meetings, clarifies the laws, and describes the process of alternatives to staff and parents
- chairs meetings, schedules the CSE meetings, and monitors procedures to ensure that students are reviewed and serviced appropriately
- is available to discuss and offer expertise and knowledge of programs, legal issues, district policies, and placement in the district and out of district programs
- facilitates and coordinates objectively the process of evaluation and service recommendations to ensure that parents' rights are not violated
- coordinates records, organizes information, and sees that students are serviced in the least restrictive environment; also sees that both student and parent rights are enforced
- brings forth the great breadth of knowledge about the process, the services, and the child in order to facilitate the coming together of professionals who must determine level of need and degree of services, if any

PARENT REACTION TO CSE

In districts that I audited, I found that approximately 70% of parents commented positively about their dealings with the CSE. They described the dealings as good to excellent and characterized the members of the CSE as sensitive, friendly, and helpful. Here are examples of what you can expect parents to state;

- I feel the communication lines are open. I am always able to get an answer.
- I feel they have been very helpful and supportive.
- CSE members are sympathetic, accommodating, and thorough.
- We've worked pretty much together on all phases of my child's school experience.
- I am very pleased with the committee. They not only explain what I do not understand but allow me to give input on my own child and take into consideration what I've stated.
- The CSE is great; they're always there for you. Any question I have always get answered or somebody gets back to me.
- I went in feeling frightened to being made to feel very comfortable.

However, there are critics of the CSE, and their comments shed a different light on the management and operation of special education. You need to verify the concerns expressed by parents and, if they turn out to be valid, correct the problems. Here is a sample of some critical comments:

- The committee took very long to respond. They were out of compliance for both my children. But when they finally moved and I "yelled" enough, I was served.
- It took seven months to start speech. I initiated the process in 6/94 and did not get an evaluation until 2/95; speech classes didn't start then until 3/25/95.
- The experience was terrible. They have been impolite. Not sensitive to a parent's input.
- The first time I really thought that the committee was looking out for the best interest of my child. But since I got more involved, they really don't know the child's interest.

STEP 4 TO REDUCE THE SIZE OF THE STUDENT POOL

If you want to reduce the number of students classified, you need to be sure that the chair of the CSE is not yielding to enormous parental pressure, teacher/staff pressure, systematic pressures that exist within the school system itself, and private clinician pressure to classify students.

EFFECTIVE OR INEFFECTIVE GATEKEEPER

There is a serious concern regarding whether the CSE as constituted, serves as an effective gatekeeper for students. In the audits, I found that minority students were more apt to be classified than white students. Although males were more apt than females to be classified once referred, it was not true in all districts. In the districts that I audited, I found that approximately 70% to 92% of referred students were classified by the CSEs.

In one district, data indicate that 26% of students referred for evaluation were not classified. Chart 8.1A indicates that minority students, especially Latinos, once referred for placement in special education, were more apt to be classified than white students. Also, a greater percentage of female students than male students, in each ethnic/racial group, were classified, once referred for evaluation by classroom teachers. Chart 8.1A indicates the number and percent of students referred, but not classified, by ethnic group/race and gender.

Chart 8.1B indicates that 30% of students referred for evaluation were not classified in another district. A greater percent of Afro-American students than Latino and white students were classified, once referred for evaluation by classroom teachers. Also, a greater percent of male students than female students were classified, once referred for evaluation by teachers.

In another district, thirty-one (8.1%) of the 382 students referred for evaluation for placement in special education did not qualify for placement. This means that ap-

CHART 8.1A **The Number and Percent of Students Referred But Not Classified by Ethnic Group/Race and Gender (one sample).**

Ethnic/Race	Number	Percent
White	31	26
Male	25	29
Female	6	19
Afro-American	7	26
Male	5	33
Female	2	17
Latinos	3	23
Male	3	30
Female	0	0

CHART 8.1B The Number and Percent of Students Referred but Not Classified by Ethnic Group/Race and Gender (a second sample).

Ethnic/Race	Number	Percent
White		
Male	14	40
Female	6	46
Total	20	42
Afro-American		
Male	2	7
Female	3	20
Total	5	12
Latinos		
Male	1	20
Female	1	100
Total	2	33

proximately 92% of students referred were classified. Also, it was interesting that all those students that did not qualify were white. Furthermore, females (9.7) were slightly more apt than males (7.2) not to be classified. Yet psychologists insisted that the CSE is an effective "gatekeeper" for all students. They reasoned that

- We serve the needs of all students.
- The CSE tries to serve the needs of all students.
- Just as in the judicial system of this country, so too is the CSE "Blind" to such factors in deciding need and degree of services. The role of gatekeeper pertains solely to the degree of educational need!
- We try to serve the needs of all students, and we do it well.

STEP 5 TO REDUCE THE SIZE OF THE STUDENT POOL

You can reduce the number of students classified by putting in place well-defined criteria to ensure that a single standard exists and that minority students are not subject to discrimination.

SUMMARY

You now know how to audit the CSE. You know to make sure that the building principal plays a more pivotal role in the CSE. You know to question the influence of psychologists on other CSE members. And you know to be aware of the limitations of tests. More importantly, you know to check to make sure that racial/ethnic and gender issues are not factors in decisions made by the CSE to classify students.

REFERENCES

"The Role of Sex Differences in the Referral Process as Measured by the Peabody Picture Vocabulary Test—Revised and the Wechsler Intelligence Scale for Children—Revised," *Psychology in the Schools* (October 1989).

Larry P. Task Force Report: Policy and Alternative Assessment Guideline Recommendations (January 1989).

9

Minority Students

AIM

THIS chapter has a dual aim. The first is to show you how to organize your data to determine whether minority students in your school/district are dealt with in an equitable and objective manner in the referral and classification processes. The second is to share with you findings from two audits, District 1 and District 2, so that you can appreciate some of the subtleties and nuances related to the referral and classification of minority students. There are numerous charts to help you organize your data. You will notice that the matrices of terms and phrases used by the two districts differ. Also, the information is massaged differently in each district. This should help you decide on the best method to present your data. There are loads of statistics that you can use as benchmarks to evaluate your own school/district. This information should help you develop interventions to reduce the number of minority students that are referred inappropriately for special education.

THE ETHNIC-RACIAL ISSUE IN SPECIAL EDUCATION

You know that you need to address the issue of ethnic-racial imbalance in special education for at least two reasons. First, you have a responsibility to make sure that special education is not used as a "dumping ground" program for bothersome/demanding students in general and minority students specifically. Second, you need to dispel the perception among minority parents in your district that you operate a racist program. Are poor minority students assigned disproportionately to special education because their cultural street corner behavior is not understood by middle-class personnel in your school/district? You need to know whether there is an ethnic-racial imbalance in your district's referral process and, if there is an imbalance, the reasons for the imbalance.

FOUR GENERAL FINDINGS REGARDING RACE

The audits that I completed provide more data to substantiate previous findings that special education programs tend to be populated disproportionately by ethnic minority students and that the referral process is far from effective and objective. There are four general findings from my audits that you need to be aware of in order to make the referral process equitable, objective, and effective. My audits found that the

percent of minority students referred for special education always exceeded the percent of minority students enrolled in school/district by 5%–20%. However, in one case I found that the percent of Latino students referred was less than the percent of Latino students enrolled in the school/district. I have never found this to be surprising to district personnel. Does this mean that you have an insurmountable systemic problem or does this mean that you need to better educate your entire staff?

African American students, especially males, were more likely than other students to be referred for multiple reasons i.e. academic and behavioral, academic and speech and language. African American students were more likely than white students to be referred for "Speech and Language" problems. If this was your school/district you would want to know whether there is a relationship between a student's academic frustration and his/her disruptive classroom behavior.

The percent of African American females referred for evaluation within school districts for special education is more skewed than the percent of African American males referred for evaluation. Although African American males are in some cases less likely than white males to be referred for behavioral reasons, African American females are always referred more often than white females for behavioral reasons. You need to know whether the African American young women in your school/district are referred because they are handicapped or because their learned manner of dealing with frustrating situations conflicts with the values of the teachers and the norms of the class.

Committees on Special Education (CSEs) tended to be a more effective gatekeeper for white students and females than African American students and males. In one district referred African American students (88%) were more likely than white students (58%) to be classified. This phenomena was especially true for kindergarten and first grade. Seven out of 10 (70%) white students referred for evaluation in kindergarten and first grade were not classified compared to 3 out of 21 (14%) of the African American students in these grades. If these data were from your school/district you would want to know the reasons for these figures and the criteria for student placement in special education.

If these were the findings from your school/district, you would raise questions regarding teacher expectations, perceptions, and interactions with students based on race and gender. Undoubtedly, you would also initiate whatever interventions were needed or appropriate to ensure the equity, objectivity, and effectiveness of the referral process. In this case, the steps taken to remedy this problem would help to downsize and reduce special education costs.

REFERRALS BY RACE AND ETHNIC GROUP

You first need to gather baseline data about the demographics of your district in order to complete an objective analysis of the treatment of minority students in the referral and classification processes. If you follow the four steps in this chapter, you will be able to determine if the referral process and classification process in your school/district are equitable, objective, and effective. If the referral process and classification process are flawed, you will be able to identify specific flaws and take steps to correct the difficulties.

DISTRICT 1

DEMOGRAPHICS

Let us look at District 1 to see how to carry out an objective analysis of the treatment of minority students in the referral and classification processes. In District

1, of 4898 students, 13% or 632 students had been classified. In the year that the audit took place, ninety-eight students had been referred for evaluation for placement in special education. First, in order to determine whether there might be a problem in the referral process and classification process, I developed Chart 9.1. Data were gathered from my student database. Chart 9.1 indicates that a red flag needs to go up. There might be a problem with the referral process. I say *might* because I want to avoid the establishment of a quota system. However, the discrepancy between the percent of white and African Americans in the total student population, the percent of whites and African Americans referred for evaluation, and the percent of whites and African Americans classified sure raises both eyebrows. Do you know the racial/ethnic makeup of your student population? Do you know the racial/ethnic composition of students referred for evaluation for placement in special education? And do you know the racial composition of your special education program? If not, develop Chart 9.1, gather data from your student database, and determine whether your district has a problem to resolve.

AFRICAN AMERICAN

Your second step is to determine if this discrepancy is caused by events in one school or is a problem systemwide. This means that you need to gather information about minority referrals from each school in your district. All this information is readily available from the student database you developed at the start of the project. Chart 9.2 indicates that the percent of African American students referred for evaluation exceeds the percent of African American students in the district in each and every school. As a matter of fact, further analysis indicates that all the African American students referred for evaluations for special education in elementary schools 2 and 5 and the high school are all classified. Does this surprise you? Would you be surprised to find this in your own school/district? Do you know the racial/ethnic makeup of the students referred in each building in your district? If not, develop Chart 9.2, gather data from your student database, and determine whether a problem exists and, if one exists, whether it is localized or systemic.

CHART 9.1 Percent of Students by Race/Ethnicity in the Total School Population and Percent of Students by Race/Ethnicity Referred for Evaluation.

	Whites	African Americans	Latinos
Percent of total student population	68	22	9
Percent of students referred for evaluation for placement in special education	49	42	6
Percent of students classified	37	54	8

CHART 9.2 Number and Percent of African American Students Referred for Evaluation for Placement in Special Education in Each School.

School	Number of African American Students Referred in the School	Percent of Students That Were African American
Elem. 1	4	80
Elem. 2	15	63
Elem. 3	7	44
Elem. 4	4	31
Elem. 5	4	33
M.S.	5	25
H.S.	3	38

AFRICAN AMERICAN FEMALES

Your third step is to determine whether the disproportionate number of minority referrals is also a gender issue. This means that you need to gather information about minority referrals by gender in your district. All this information is readily available from the student database you developed at the start of the project. Chart 9.3 indicates that minority referrals is a serious problem for both males and females but most especially for African American females. First, African American males made up 40% of all males referred for evaluation while African American females made up 50% of all females referred for evaluation. Second, African American females made up 38% of all African Americans referred for evaluation while white females made up 27% of all white students referred for evaluation. Are you surprised by the percent of young African Americans referred for evaluation? Do you have any ideas why African American students, especially African American females, have so much difficulty in school? The first step that you need to take to unravel this mystery is to develop Chart 9.3, gather data from your student database, and determine whether a problem exists and if the problem is also one that involves gender.

TERMS/PHRASES USED IN REFERRALS BY RACIAL/ETHNIC GROUP BY GENDER

Your fourth step is to determine the reasons for the referrals of minority students by gender. Chart 9.4 indicates the terms/phrases used by classroom teachers

on forms to refer students for evaluation for placement in special education. All this information is readily available from the student database you developed at the start of the project. This information helps you to identify the reasons that students are referred and enables you to determine objectively whether referrals are based upon race/ethnicity and gender.

Chart 9.4 indicates that, in District 1, minority students are more apt than white students to have "academic" and "speech and language" problems. Both minority and white students are referred for "behavioral" reasons at approximately the same percent. Chart 9.4 indicates that both African American males and females have a difficult time with the norms/expectations set by classroom teachers. However, Chart 9.4 provides you with a wealth of practical and usable information about minority referrals. Here are examples of the information you can get from Chart 9.4:

(1) Classroom teacher referrals of African American students placed equal weight for both males (53%) and females (56%) on "academic" problems. Males (23%) were referred more often than females (17%) for "behavioral" reasons. Also, males (16%) were referred more often than females (11%) for "speech and language" problems.

(2) White male students (57%) were slightly more apt to be referred for evaluation for "academic" reasons than African American male students (54%); but white female students (75%) were more apt to be referred for evaluation for "academic" reasons than African American female students (53%).

CHART 9.3 Number of Referrals by Race/Ethnic Group and Gender.

Gender	White	African American	Latinos	Other
Male	35	27	5	1
Female	13	15	1	1
Total	48	42	6	2

CHART 9.4 **Number of Times Terms/Phrases/Words Used in Referrals by Ethnic/Racial Group and Gender.**

Codes	Terms	White		African American		Latino	
		Male	Female	Male	Female	Male	Female
	Academics						
A01	Not able to master curriculum				1		
A02	Lack of progress academically			1			1
A03	Organizational skill	1		1			
A04	Low academic performance	7	7	7	5	1	
A05	Failing or below average work academically	2		3	1		
A06	Academic weakness significant	1			1		
A07	Poor classroom performance			1			
A08	Academic difficulties	4		2	2	1	
A09	Difficulties in reading, math and writing skills	1		1		1	
A10	Difficulty in reading and language expression			1		1	
A11	Receptive understanding seems low			1			
A12	Difficulty understanding what he reads	1					
A13	Reading skills 2–3 years below level			1			
A14	Difficulties in reading	1		1			
A15	Difficulty completing grade-level work independently	1					
A16	Difficulty grasping and retaining information			1			
A17	Difficulties in all academic areas					1	
A18	Below grade level in reading skills, written language, and math	2					
A19	Weakness in following directions	1					
A20	Poor writing skills	1					
A21	Difficulty applying math concepts	1					
A22	Low vocabulary level		1				
A23	Difficulty with recall of literal information		1				
A24	Difficulties with details of written and spoken language		1				
A25	Difficulties following directions or staying on task and expressing ideas			1			
A26	Significant discrepancy between ability levels in math and language		1				
A27	Nonreader		1				
A28	Academic frustration	1					
A29	Poor reading skills	1					
A30	Math skills			1			
	Subtotal	26	12	23	10	5	1
	Behavior						
B01	Attention skills			2			
B02	Emotional outbursts			1			
B03	Negative and inappropriate behavior	1		1			
B04	Unusual behavior	1					
B05	Defiant manner	1					
B06	Unhappy and hostile boy			1			
B07	Bit his arm	1					
B08	Mute with adults	1					
B09	Unable to form any friendships			1			
B10	Emotional stability questionable			1			
B11	Short attention span	1					

CHART 9.4 (continued).

Codes	Terms	White		African American		Latino	
		Male	Female	Male	Female	Male	Female
	Behavior						
B12	Aggressive and disruptive classroom behavior			1			
B13	When frustrated academically, acting up behavior	1					
B14	Immature	1		1			
B15	Socially maladjusted				1		
B16	Depression and medical factors		1				
B17	Behavioral control difficulty	4					
B18	Difficulty respecting and obeying authority figures			1		1	
B19	Acts out frequently					1	
B20	Suicidal	1			1		
B21	Hostile and threatening tone	1					
B22	Attention deficit	1					
	Subtotal	15	1	10	3	2	0
	Speech and Hearing						
C01	Difficult time pronouncing words correctly and poor language development				1		
C02	Possible language deficiency			1			
C03	Language delay possible			1			
C04	Poor articulation and limited speech	1					
C05	Speech difficulties	1					
C06	Poor speech and language skills			2	1		
C07	Concern over a lack of verbal expression			1			
C08	Language difficulties			1		1	
C09	Poor oral expression skills			1			
C10	Speech difficult to understand					1	
	Subtotal	2	0	7	2	2	0
	Other						
D01	Fine motor skills are poor			2			
D02	Pediatrician recommended testing because of surgery at age 5	1					
D03	Poor visual motor skills			1			
D04	Moved before testing		1				
D05	Recommendation of court	1	1		1		
D06	Refuse to come to school/truant		1		1		
D07	Attempt to run away from home				1		
D08	Quadriplegic	1					
	Subtotal	3	3	3	3	0	0
	Total	46	16	43	18	9	1

CHART 9.5 Percent of Students by Race/Ethnicity in the Total School Population and Percent of Students by Race/Ethnicity Referred for Evaluation.

	Whites	African American	Latinos
Percent of total student population	84	12	4
Percent of students referred for evaluation for placement in special education	73	17	10

(3) White male students (33%) were more apt to be referred for "behavioral" reasons than African American students (23%), but African American females (17%) were nearly three times as likely to be referred for "behavioral" reasons as white female students (6%).

(4) Six Latino students were referred for evaluation for special education. The lone female was referred because of "lack of progress academically." "Academic" reasons accounted for 56% of the referrals for Latino males (five out of nine males). Latino males were referred 22% of the time for "behavioral" and "speech and language" reasons.

DISTRICT 2

Let us look at District 2 to see how to carry out an objective analysis of the treatment of minority students in the referral and classification processes. As you read this section, you will see the wealth of information you can gather through this process to better ensure the equity, objectivity, and effectiveness of the referral process. There are some modifications in the way these data are massaged and presented as compared with data from District 1.

First you need to provide a picture of student enrollment by race/ethnicity in District 2. You should point out that 14% (1223) of the district's 8468 students were classified. In the year that the audit was completed, information was gathered on 159 out of 322 students referred for special education.

First, in order to determine whether there might be a problem in the referral process, I developed Chart 9.5. Data was gathered from my student database. Chart 9.5 indicates that a red flag needs to go up. There might be a problem with the referral process. I say *might* because I want to avoid the establishment of a quota system. However, the discrepancy between the percent of white and African Americans in the total student population and the percent of whites and African Americans referred for evaluation raises at least one eyebrow.

REFERRALS BY GENDER

Second, you need to help the reader to see some patterns in the referral process. Chart 9.6 indicates that 71% of students referred for evaluation are males and 29% are females. However, you might find it interesting to know that, in District 2 schools, where a greater percent of teachers earned credits in special education courses and indicated that they hoped to gain educational suggestions from referring students for evaluation, there is a more balanced division of referrals between male and female. Is this the case in your school? Does this mean that you need to inservice classroom teachers about special education? Do you need to point out the need to classroom teachers to use a consistent criteria for the referral of females and males for special education?

TERMS/PHRASES USED IN REFERRALS BY GENDER

You know that an analysis of terms/phrases used by classroom teachers to refer students provides a series

CHART 9.6 Referrals by Gender by School.

School	Female	Male	Total
Elem. 1	3	8	11
Elem. 2	12	33	45
Elem. 3	12	17	29
Elem. 4	7	9	16
M.S.	3	23	26
J.H.S.	8	10	18
H.S.	1	13	14
Total	46	113	159

of snapshots of reasons for referrals. These snapshots are particularly revealing when it comes to an evaluation about reasons for the referral of minority students in District 2. A review of terms/phrases used in referrals indicates that teachers cited academic problems more often than other reasons for referring both males and females for evaluations. Chart 9.7 indicates that

- Academic terms were used equally for males (47%) and females(46%).
- Males (32%) were referred more often for behavioral problems than females (22%).
- Males were referred for speech and hearing problems (14%) less often than females (20%).

CLASSIFICATION OF AFRICAN AMERICAN STUDENTS

Chart 9.8 indicates that the percent of classified African American students in District 2 exceeds the percent of African American students in five out of seven schools by 20% to 100%. Only in the high school is the percent of classified African American students less than the percent of enrolled African American students. What is the reason for the lower percent of classified minority students in the high school?

AFRICAN AMERICAN FEMALES

Notice that Chart 9.9 indicates that African American females are the most disproportionately referred students in District 2. After all, African American males made up 13% of all males referred for evaluation, while African American females made up 26% of all females referred for evaluation. Also, African American females made up 44% of all African Americans referred for evaluation while white females made up 26% of all white students referred for evaluation. Do you have any explanation for this picture? How can you use this information to reduce the number of African American females referred for special education in your district?

You need to know that the administrators, psychologists, and members of the CSEs are overwhelmingly white in District 2. There are ten school administrators; nine are white males and one is an African American female. There are seven psychologists, five being white males, one a white female, and one an African American male. There are forty nonadministrative members of building CSEs. Ten are white males, twenty-nine are white females, and one is an African American female. Does the race/ethnicity of administrators, psychologists, and

CSE members influence classification decisions? Does it influence decisions in your school/district? What steps can you take to remedy this situation if it exists in your district?

As you ponder this information, remember the questions raised about

- the objectivity of classification criteria/standards
- differences between demanding/bothersome students and handicapped students
- differences between low-achieving students and learning disabled students
- test bias and the Larry P case
- the integrity of school psychologists

How sure would you be that all the referred and classified minority and majority students in your district are, in fact, handicapped and had to be classified? Who do you have in your district that is specifically an advocate for students in general and especially for minority students?

Chart 9.10 indicates that similar reasons were given for the referrals of African American males and females. However, when data from Chart 9.10 are used in conjunction with Chart 9.8 it is clear that

- White male students (48%) are more likely to be referred for evaluation for academic reasons than African American male students (38%), and white female students (52%) are more apt to be referred for evaluation for academic reasons than African American female students (35%).
- African American females (35%) are more than twice as likely to be referred for behavioral reasons as white female students (15%).

LATINOS

Once again, you need to keep in mind that there is not a sufficient number of Latino students in this audit to generalize any findings; however, the results of this audit do suggest that, if inequities can occur in District 2, they may also be occurring in your school/district. Chart 9.11 indicates that Latino males are more apt than Latino females to be referred for evaluation for academic and behavioral reasons. However, when data from Chart 9.11 are used with Charts 9.7 and 9.10, it is clear that

- Latino male (56%) students are more apt to be referred for evaluation for academic reasons than either white (48%) or African American (38%) male students, and Latino (0%) females

CHART 9.7 **Number of Times Buzzwords Used in Referrals by Gender.**

Codes	Terms	Male	Female
	Academic		
2	Testing	1	1
3	Didn't master skill	1	
4	Can't follow directions	6	2
9	Almost nonverbal	2	
10	Unable to do work	1	
11	Lacks background	1	
13	Below grade level	4	3
15	Work sloppy	1	
19	Academic problem	12	3
22	Poor academic level	1	2
26	Low academic achievement	5	
28	Behind with work	1	
29	Not able to handle work	1	
30	Learning difficulties	3	1
32	Cannot recognize letters	1	3
35	Poor comprehension	2	2
37	Difficulty in math	6	3
38	Can't spell new words	3	
40	CAT test low	1	1
41	Failed DIAL test	3	
47	Poor retention	1	
49	Low-level conceptual development	1	
51	Test scores 3 years below		1
52	Difficulty completing assignment	1	
56	Unable to see cause/effect	1	
62	Failed courses	1	1
71	Difficulty taking tests	1	
	Subtotal	62	23
	Behavior		
5	Attention deficit	8	4
6	Threatens peers	1	
12	Outburst and cries	1	1
17	Poor behavior	8	1
20	Behavioral concerns	6	
21	Poor performance	7	2
24	Antagonistic behavior	2	2
25	Can be violent	1	
54	Attention disorders	1	
55	Dangerous and disruptive	1	
58	Quiet in class		1
61	Lack of social maturity	1	
64	Aggressive/disruptive	1	
65	Very active	1	
69	Poor peer relationships	2	
73	Immature	1	
74	Emotional problems	1	
	Subtotal	43	11

CHART 9.7 (continued).

Codes	Terms	Male	Female
	Speech and Hearing		
1	Hearing problem		2
7	Trouble expressing		1
8	Doesn't speak often		1
14	Poor language mechanics	1	
18	Speech unintelligible	2	1
27	Suspected auditorial placement	1	
31	Mispronounces words		1
33	Speech therapy		1
34	Doesn't speak in complete sentences	1	1
36	Limited vocabulary	1	
42	Problem with articulation	5	
45	Speech skills	1	
48	Immature speech	1	
50	Mild fluency problem	1	
53	Speech interfering with others	1	
57	Speech problem	1	1
60	Hearing aid	1	
63	Difficult to understand		1
66	Speech articulation dysfluencies	1	
75	Language processing deficiency	1	
	Subtotal	19	10
	Other		
16	Poor motor control	1	1
23	Parental frustration		1
44	Unmotivated	1	
46	Prior special education	2	
59	Frustrated	1	
67	Parental request	2	3
68	Chapter 1 teacher concern	1	
70	Absenteeism	1	
72	Request for mainstreaming		1
	Subtotal	9	6
	Total	133	50

CHART 9.8 Percent of African American Students in School Compared to the Percent of African American Students in Special Education Programs at the Start of the Study.

School	Percent of African American Students in the School	Percent of African American Students in Special Education
Elem. 1	7	14
Elem. 2	16	16
Elem. 3	8	11
Elem. 4	15	18
M.S.	13	20
J.H.S.	15	17
H.S.	13	9

CHART 9.9 **Number of Referrals by Race/Ethnic Group and Gender.**

Gender	White	African American	Latinos	Other
Male	87	15	10	1
Female	31	12	3	0
Total	118	27	13	1

CHART 9.10 **Number of Times Terms/Phrases Used in Referrals of African American Students by Gender.**

Codes	Terms	Male	Female
	Academic		
2	Testing		1
3	Didn't master skill	1	
4	Can't follow directions	1	
10	Unable to do work	1	
11	Lacks background	1	
13	Below grade level		1
19	Academic problem	1	
32	Cannot recognize letters		2
37	Difficulty in math		1
49	Low-level conceptual development	1	
51	Test scores 3 years below		1
	Subtotal	6	6
	Behavior		
5	Attention deficit	2	2
6	Threatens peers	1	
12	Outburst and cries		1
17	Poor behavior	2	1
21	Poor performance	1	
24	Antagonistic behavior		2
	Subtotal	6	6
	Speech and Hearing		
1	Hearing problems		1
7	Trouble expressing		1
8	Doesn't speak often		1
27	Suspected auditorial placement	1	
34	Doesn't speak in complete sentences	1	1
42	Problem with articulation	1	
48	Immature speech	1	
	Subtotal	4	4
	Other		
16	Poor motor control		1
	Subtotal	0	1
	Total	16	17

CHART 9.11 Number of Times Terms/Phrases Used in Referrals of Latino Students by Gender.

Codes	Terms	Male	Female
	Academic		
13	Below grade level	2	
15	Work sloppy	1	
19	Academic problem	2	
22	Poor academic level	2	
38	Can't spell new words	1	
71	Difficulty taking tests	1	
	Subtotal	9	0
	Behavior		
5	Attention deficit	1	
17	Poor behavior	2	
20	Behavioral concerns	1	
58	Quiet in class		1
	Subtotal	4	1
	Speech and Hearing		
36	Limited vocabulary	1	
57	Speech problems		1
75	Language processing deficiency	1	
	Subtotal	2	1
	Other		
16	Poor motor control	1	
67	Parental request		1
	Subtotal	1	1
	Total	16	3

are less apt to be referred for evaluation for academic reasons than either white (52%) or African American (35%) female students.
- Latino males (25%) are less likely than African American (38%) and white (29%) male students to be referred for behavioral reasons.

SUMMARY

You have seen a wealth of information that an audit of the referral process provides about race and gender in your district. With this information in hand, you can develop strategies and interventions to remedy the racial and gender inequities in the referral process. For example, you might want to counsel all students, including minority females, about the appropriate way to express their academic frustrations or displeasure with students or classroom teachers in your school/district. By the same token, you might decide that some or all classroom teachers need to be inserviced about the ways some students, including minority females, deal with frustration and displeasure. Undoubtedly, this will help to reduce the pool of students referred for special education. You are now aware of even more substantive issues such as the criteria for classification, test bias, and cultural and socioeconomic differences between classroom teachers and poor minority students that may result in racial imbalance in your special education program.

10

Supervision of Special Education Personnel: More Effective and Efficient Use of Teaching Assistants, Psychologists, Social Workers, and LD Teacher-Consultants

AIM

THIS chapter helps you to improve the supervision of special education by analyzing the efficiency and cost-effectiveness of teaching assistants, psychologists, social workers, and LD teacher-consultants. A review of perceptions of special education teachers and principals makes it clear that there is a need to define clearly the roles of the director of special education and principals in the supervision of special education teachers. There is a series of questions that indicate the steps you need to take to coordinate the efforts of the director of special education and principals in the supervision of special education teachers. You are shown how to determine whether teaching assistants are used appropriately and whether psychologists, social workers, and LD teacher-consultants use their time effectively and efficiently. There are two charts and a number of steps spelled out to help you better use special education support personnel effectively and cost-efficiently.

INTRODUCTION

You are likely to find the information in this chapter upsetting, but necessary, if you want to ensure the effectiveness and cost-efficiency of the special education program. This chapter supplies an album of snapshots that shows that there is confusion in some districts about the roles of directors of special education, principals, and department chairpersons in the supervision of special education personnel. These snapshots show that the actual supervision of special education teachers and support personnel (i.e., teaching assistants, psychologists, social workers, and LD teacher-consultants), in some districts, is, at best, slipshod and disjointed and, at worst, neglected and nonexistent. In all cases where this exists, the school/district is not getting the bang for its bucks that the community has a right to expect. Therefore, you need to be sure that supervisors

are fulfilling their responsibilities and that they have ensured that special education personnel are used effectively and cost-efficiently.

ORGANIZATIONAL STRUCTURE OF SPECIAL EDUCATION

BACKGROUND

You need to know that there are many different types of organizational structures for special education services, and at times, this affects the supervision of special education personnel. Some organizational structures make a great deal of sense. Other times, they mirror financial cutbacks or, more appropriately, the attempt of district personnel to have the same number of tasks performed by fewer and fewer administrators/supervisors. Oftentimes, special education is part of pupil personnel services. Sometimes, it is under the direction of the assistant superintendent for curriculum and instruction. Once in a while it is linked with personnel. Most of the time, special education directors have responsibilities for all special education teachers and support personnel. Other times, these responsibilities are divided between special education directors and other management and supervisory personnel. Most of the time, the number of supervisors for the special education program is adequate. Other times, there is a lack of adequate supervisory personnel. However, I have found few special education programs, regardless of organizational structure, supervisory responsibilities, or size of program, that utilize special education personnel effectively and cost-efficiently.

RESPONSIBILITIES OF DIRECTORS OF SPECIAL EDUCATION

You have heard the special education director's

mantra repeated six times a day in the direction of the superintendent's office: "I'm overworked, I have too many things to do, I have to run, I need help." Is this true and is it a reasonable response from a competent and capable director? Or is this the cry used by a special education director whose program is disorganized and whose personnel are utilized poorly?

You will find that the responsibilities for a director of special education can be so broad that they include more than managing and supervising special education teachers and serving as chair of the committee on special education. In addition to supervision of special education teachers, the director of special education may be responsible for evaluations of youngsters, teaching assistants, psychologists, social workers, speech therapists, home teaching, transportation, and placement of students outside the district. In all cases, the director of special education shares supervisory responsibilities for special education teachers with building principals and, in some instances on the secondary level, with subject matter department chairpersons. However, I have found that, in some districts, the director of special education is unable to carry out all his/her responsibilities effectively. Sometimes, this is due to the size of the special education program. Other times, this is due to the lack of a coordinated effort by the director and principals and/or chairpersons to supervise special education teachers. Once in a while, it is due to incompetence. In every instance, when the director of special education is unable to carry out his/her responsibilities, it means that district money has been used poorly.

Directors of special education are responsible for the daily operations of special education. You might find it helpful to know how at least one other director of special education spends his/her time so that you can compare his/her time management with that of your director of special education. In one audit, I found that the director of special education allocates 35% of his/her time to student services; 30% to supervision of special education; 25% to serving as a resource/liaison; 5% to reporting, budget, and finance. If the director of special education is unable to complete all of his/her responsibilities, is it possible that it is due to poor time management rather than the size of the district or the assigned tasks? How effectively does your director of special education manage his/her time?

THE VIEWS OF SPECIAL EDUCATION TEACHERS ON SUPERVISION BY PRINCIPALS AND SPECIAL EDUCATION DIRECTORS

Based on information gathered from special education teachers and principals, I found that special educa-tion teachers are not supervised effectively. This is, in part, because the supervisory responsibilities of the director of special education and principals are either not spelled out clearly and/or are not well coordinated. Are the supervisory tasks of the director of special education and principals in your district spelled out clearly and well coordinated?

In my audits, I found that, generally, special education teachers indicate that both principals and Directors of special education are supportive of staff, actively involved in formal and informal observations, and concerned about supplies and materials. However, special education teachers picture principals as more involved with administrative functions and directors of special education as part of a resource support system. Special education teachers indicate that principals are more likely than the director of special education to be involved with student discipline, scheduling, team meetings, and the monitoring of plan books. On the other hand, the director of special education is thought to have a greater involvement than principals in the areas of student placement, parent and teacher conferences, and grade level meetings. Special education teachers point out that directors of special education oversee the entire special education program, plan, design and implement staff development programs, and brainstorm with staff.

SUPERVISION OF SPECIAL EDUCATION TEACHERS

Just as the old adage points out that one cannot be a little bit pregnant, so too you cannot have some supervision of special education teachers. Either all special education teachers are supervised by the principal or the director of special education alone or together in a well-coordinated program of supervision, or the program lacks supervision. As a result of my audits, I found that there are some principals that supervise and some principals that do not supervise special education teachers. In most cases, I found that there are not well-coordinated plans of supervision implemented by principals and the director of special education. Do the principals in your district supervise special education teachers? Do they coordinate their activities with the director of special education?

SPECIAL EDUCATION TEACHERS' PERCEPTIONS OF THE ROLES OF PRINCIPALS IN THE SUPERVISION OF SPECIAL EDUCATION

You are likely to find that perceptions of the role of principals in your district vary based on either the teaching assignments and/or the grade level of special education teachers. Special education teachers who instruct 15:1 classes have more positive comments about principals than special education teachers of 5:1 classes. Also, secondary special education teachers have more positive comments about principals than elementary special education teachers. Here are some examples of their comments, which range on a continuum of general support to specific and detailed tasks performed by principals. They indicate that their principal

- is always available and his door is always open to offer support and formal/informal assessment
- lends support with problems needing the intervention of higher authority
- actively observes students both formally and informally and presides over weekly team meetings
- sets up teams and a consultant teacher model
- is part of a team—he/she assists in handling problems
- is familiar with the students and their needs; disciplines and supports students; also outlines curriculum, provides material, and acts as an advocate
- sets the guidelines and working atmosphere for the building; is supportive of special education and is always there if needed for support
- is active in all our team meetings and in making decisions for each child individually
- gives me the time and attention needed to correct problems
- checks planbooks, observes, visits, and sets up testing schedules
- is involved with scheduling, supplies and materials, parent and student meetings, and placement decisions
- makes formal and informal observations, collects planbooks, attends team and grade level meetings, and offers support with discipline
- assists with discipline
- monitors planbooks and curriculum
- assists with questions and problems, counsels and/or disciplines students, brainstorms on policy, and observes classes

Some special education teachers in your district are likely to be less than enthusiastic about the role of principals in supervising their classes. In my audits, I found that many special education teachers that are critical of principals have 5:1 assignments. Some special education teachers indicate that their principals have no role or a very little role in supervising their special education classes. Samples of their comments include

- The principal is rarely seen in the classroom and has little to no role in supervising the class.
- Besides scheduling and discipline, there is very little interaction with the resource room classes.
- Many principals do not understand the role of the teacher and/or the special education program; therefore, they often entrust the teacher to make decisions or suggest they contact the special education administrator.
- The principal is always available for help and support if it is needed. Usually, it is not needed.

VIEWS OF PRINCIPALS ON THEIR ROLE IN SUPERVISING SPECIAL EDUCATION TEACHERS

You are likely to find that perceptions of principals in your district on their roles in supervising special education teachers covers the complete continuum from active involvement to passive detachment. Most principals are of the opinion that they are involved on a daily basis with special education teachers in the same manner that they are with all teachers. Others are candid about their lack of knowledge and/or involvement. Here is a sample of comments by principals:

- My role in supervising, monitoring, and evaluating special education curriculum was the same as it was for all subjects taught in that school. I monitor planbooks to evaluate the nature of the delivery of curriculum and instruction. This helps me to ensure that students in special education classes cover the same material as students in mainstream classes.
- The supervision of special education teachers is not any different from the regular population. I have had no input regarding special education curriculum.
- I have formally observed all special education teachers one time and have made numerous informal observations of staff and students. In addition, classroom teachers and special education teachers meet individually with me to solve problems.
- I check planbooks once a week.
- I am involved on a day-to-day basis—observing informally and formally, reading planbooks, meeting with teachers about mainstreaming and suggesting appropriate materials and strategies for students.
- In past years, I had observed all special education teachers at least once a year. This year, I made two formal and four informal observations. My assistant observed two special education teachers formally. Between

us, we held five special education department meetings.

- I play an insignificant role in supervising, monitoring, and evaluating special education curriculum. I am not sure what special education students are taught.

- I do not have a handle on the curriculum. I think the program is weak in content and that the teachers need to improve their classroom management skills. Most of the time I spend on discipline centers on special education children.

- I think that there is some curriculum in place. However, it is not updated. I question the quality of the work. I doubt whether the curriculum that exists is useful to teachers, and I am appalled by the fact that the special education program uses worksheets.

STEPS FOR PRINCIPALS TO TAKE TO IMPROVE SUPERVISION OF SPECIAL EDUCATION TEACHERS

The first step to take to improve the supervision of special education teachers is to spell out the role of the principal in the supervisory process. How many formal and informal observations of special education teachers do you want principals to make? Do you want principals to observe all or some special education teachers? If you want them to observe some special education teachers, who determines which special education teachers? Do you want to have the principal coordinate all observations with the director of special education? Do you want the principal to have access to all observations of special education teachers made by the director of special education? Do you want principals to monitor planbooks and, if so, how frequently? The second step is for principals to be inserviced about special education curriculum. What is the scope and sequence of the special education curriculum? Would your principals know the breadth and depth of different special education programs? To what degree is there linkage between the special education and general curriculum? The third step is for principals to learn about strategies used by special education teachers to deliver programs. What are the strategies to use with different students? How can you observe and evaluate the effectiveness of special education teachers if you do not know their rationales for selecting specific activities?

DIRECTOR OF SPECIAL EDUCATION

I suspect that there is an eleventh commandment that most special education teachers observe regarding the director of special education. They speak only positively about the director of special education when they speak to outsiders. You are likely to find that they empathize with the director's heavy workload, are aware of the director's role in setting up special education classes and scheduling students, value his/her advice, and report that the director observes classes and teachers. However, you need to separate perception from fact; therefore, you need to listen to the perceptions of special education teachers and principals and analyze the available hard data related to the tasks of the director of special education.

Often, when I spoke with special education teachers, teaching assistants, psychologists, speech therapists, and social workers, I had the feeling that they approached the nonspecial education community as a hostile force. These were people who questioned their work, wanted to cut funds, and longed to downsize the program. Periodically, it seemed that these feelings were encouraged and manipulated by the director of special education. Sometimes, I thought that the director was viewed as a benevolent dictator, one that they would rather put up with than chance the unknown. And so they put the wagons in a circle and defended the director of special education as a means of protecting their programs and positions.

I have dealt with a number of highly ethical and professional directors of special education, and I suspect that there are legions of top flight directors of special education in the field. But I have seen a number of directors of special education rally special education parent teacher association (SEPTA) members to stonewall any modification of the special education program. Although many of these parents had students that were more severely handicapped than the bulk of the students in special education and the proposed changes would not affect adversely their children's programs, the directors did nothing to point this fact out to the parents. In some instances, I have seen directors of special education rally special education support personnel to meetings of boards of education to protest modifications in the program when, in fact, the presentations related to the supervision of the program. As a matter of fact, at one meeting, I sat facing the members of the board of education as I presented audit findings that pointed out problems with the supervision of the special education program. This meant that I sat with my back to an audience of special education personnel that thought that the presentation questioned their competence. As my report unfolded, I am sure that they realized that they had been duped by the director of special education. However, I was glad that my wife sat between the audience and my back. After all, one of us had to live to take care of the kids.

SPECIAL EDUCATION TEACHERS' PERCEPTIONS OF THE ROLES OF THE DIRECTORS OF SPECIAL EDUCATION IN THE SUPERVISION OF SPECIAL EDUCATION

Your special education teachers probably have positive views about your director of special education. After all, directors of special education are perceived as intimately involved with every aspect of the program but overworked by virtually every special education staff member, regardless of class assignments. Special education teachers point out that directors of special education

- are grossly overworked and have very little time for active supervision; however, the director is always available immediately when needed for suggestions and advice
- set up guidelines for the resource room program; is always there for any question and will return calls, even at night to discuss any problem that might come up; because there is only one director it is impossible for the him/her to spend any length of time in an individual classroom unless there is a specific problem
- has a major role to help set up the class structure and arrange for the placement of students; conducts department meeting, observes, and visits classes
- observes classes, is an integral part of the supervisory personnel; assists in problem solving; provides guidance in situations; is part of a support and resource team
- oversees the program as a whole; maintains a knowledgeable professional staff to impart appropriate instruction
- plays a very important role, observing both teacher and teacher assistant, as well as being available to answer any and all questions or concerns; has a door that is always open
- addresses legal issues, district policies, placement of students, monitoring class makeup, facilitating interaction with new students, staff communication, student observations and evaluations, parent conferences, transportation, planning of special events, coordinating medical and physical needs of students and brainstorming of specific strategies

You are likely to find some heretics, some special education teachers in your district that are less than enthusiastic about the role of director of special education in supervising their classes. Here are samples of comments of the small number of special education

teachers who are critical of directors of special education. They think that the director of special education:

- forms the classes and is there for consultation should the need arise
- has virtually had little to no role in supervising the class; provides no real direction for teachers other than providing the IEP manuals
- usually plays no role
- plays a minor role in supervising my class

PRINCIPALS' PERCEPTIONS OF THE ROLE OF THE DIRECTORS OF SPECIAL EDUCATION

You need to be aware that perceptions held by principals about the role of the director of special education vary considerably. Some principals will point out the administrative and supervisory responsibilities of directors of special education. Other principals claim that they do not know anything about the responsibilities of directors of special education. Here are samples of comments of principals about the roles of directors of special education. Principals think

- The director of special education is available for consultation. The director observes formally and informally each year. The director's expertise is tapped for curriculum and classroom management, as well as student appropriateness of placement.
- The director of special education does formal observations for all untenured staff—informal on occasion. The biggest limitation here is the huge number of staff.
- I do not know about the actions of the director.
- I do not know the director's role in supervising special education classes.
- The director has not observed any teachers up to the date of the interview.

STEPS FOR PRINCIPALS TO TAKE TO IMPROVE SUPERVISION OF SPECIAL EDUCATION TEACHERS

The first step to take to improve the supervision of special education teachers is to spell out the role of the director of special education in the supervisory process. How many formal and informal observations of special education teachers do you want the director of special education to make? Do you want the director to share observation responsibilities with principals and chairpersons? Do you want the director of special education to have access to all observations of special education teachers completed by principals? Should a principal know whether his/her special education staff has been observed by the director of special education? Do you want the director or the principals or both to monitor planbooks and, if so, how frequently?

SUPERVISION OF SUPPORT PERSONNEL

In some districts, the director of special education has supervisory responsibilities for teaching assistants, psychologists, social workers, and LD teacher-consultants. The various audits that I completed indicate that, in some instances, the director of special education does not supervise these positions effectively and that there is minimal accountability by support personnel.

All of the hard data was gathered through a curriculum mapping process. In this process, teaching assistants, psychologists, social workers, and LD teacher-consultants log the time they spend, in minutes, either daily or weekly, on a map that has a customized matrix of tasks. This map is developed by supervisory staff and the appropriate support staff. The data is entered into a software program CMT: FOR TEACHERS. The reports generated compile the time each person and then all people, by position, spend on each task. Also, the program generates reports that clarify the time required by a number of people in different positions to complete a common task, i.e., evaluation of a student.

TEACHING ASSISTANTS

I use the curriculum mapping software CMT: FOR TEACHERS to verify whether special education departments utilize their personnel properly, especially their teaching assistants and aides. One district hired seventy full-time teaching assistants at a cost of $1,057,136 to help in the delivery of the special education program. According to the New York Commissioner's Regulations (Chapter II 80.33), the duties of the teaching assistants are:

(1) Working with individual pupils or groups of pupils on special education projects
(2) Providing the teacher with information about pupils, which will assist the teacher in the development of appropriate learning experiences
(3) Assisting pupils in the use of available instructional resources and assisting in the development of instructional materials
(4) Utilizing their own special skills and abilities by assisting in instructional programs in such areas as foreign languages, arts, crafts, music, and similar subjects

(5) Assisting in related instructional work as required

ANECDOTAL COMMENTS BY SPECIAL EDUCATION TEACHERS ABOUT TEACHING ASSISTANTS

All special education teachers that worked with teacher assistants thought highly of them. Terms used to describe teaching assistants included "vital to the class," "right hand," "extra set of hands," and "shares all responsibilities." Special education teachers indicated the various tasks completed by teaching assistants that made them indispensable. Here are sample comments of special education teachers.

- The tasks of my teaching assistant included teaching small- and large-group lessons, discipline, preparing activities, supervising students, grading papers, interfacing with faculty, participating in conferences with staff and parents, collaborating with planning, lunch duty, bus duty, substituting, giving input for reports and report cards, and room organization.
- My assistant helps to instruct the children (under my direction, lessons planned by me), assists during whole class lessons, runs off dittos, stays with the class during specials (art, music, library), helps when children need to be supervised to go to other areas of the building (e.g. nurse, speech, OT, PT, etc.) and basically helps me keep my classroom running smoothly.
- In order to individualize as much as possible, my T.A. is responsible for small-group instruction with three different levels of math, spelling, and reading groups—individualized instruction, mainstream support instruction, and helping to meet individual emotional, social, and academic needs on a daily basis.
- My teaching assistant is a teacher in my classroom. She plans and implements large- and small-group lessons and provides 1:1 assistance to those in need. She also takes care of discipline, takes over the class in my place whenever necessary, and provides tutorial support for mainstreamed students. Likewise, she is called upon to cover classes of teachers reporting to the CSE.
- She works in small groups, tutors, gives students time to get control of good behaviors, plans, grades, models appropriate pro-social behavior, gives attention to students in crisis, and helps with problems that occur because of increased student-teacher ratios.
- My teaching assistant gives individualized instruction, designs special projects, teaches

groups within the class (especially when two or more subjects are taught the same period), grades student work, performs various paperwork functions (copies, testing, reports, etc.), assists with behavioral problems, and covers class when teacher pulled out (for meeting or problem).

- My teaching assistant is very important to the students and myself. The teaching assistant helps in small-group instruction, instructs students who have been absent, goes in with students to nonacademic area with regular teacher, substitutes if I am absent or at a meeting, and assists with clerical tasks (i.e., grading, xeroxing).

ANECDOTAL COMMENTS BY PRINCIPALS ABOUT TEACHING ASSISTANTS

You are likely to find that your principals mirror the thoughts of special education teachers. In one audit, principals thought that teaching assistants are "extremely valuable," "essential," "critical," and "necessary." Principals indicate that teaching assistants

- do many tasks a regular teacher performs, including supervision, clerical tasks, one-on-one supervision and tutoring
- work with students individually and in small groups to reinforce the teacher's lessons and work with behavior modification
- assist the teacher; offer individualized or small-group help; assist with discipline, time out, parent contacts
- individualize instruction and remediation; very much add their personal talents to an enriching atmosphere
- provide small-group instruction (within a

group), team teaching, and substitute for classroom teachers

THE ACTUAL USE OF TEACHING ASSISTANTS

In order to determine whether the teaching assistants spend their time on the activities spelled out in the commissioner's regulations, the district had sixty-three teaching assistants map time spent on activities at work for a two-week period. Of the sixty-three maps submitted, forty-nine were usable. Chart 10.1 indicates that the teaching assistants spent approximately 60% of their time on duties identified in the commissioner's regulations. This included time (317 minutes, or 9%) spent on preparation. However, time spent substituting, time spent on lunch, and dismissal duties were not mentioned as part of the duties by the commissioner's regulations. They spent another 10% of their time on administrative work. If you think that administrative work meets the letter and spirit of the commissioner's regulations, then 70% of the time of teaching assistants is spent appropriately. This means that, in this district, approximately $317,000 is used in ways other than suggested by the commissioner's regulations.

It is interesting to note that, in this district, there is no district policy regarding observations of teaching assistants although all were to be evaluated by the director of special education. You need to know that members of the special education task force (SETF) made every effort to justify the teaching assistants. As a result of this experience, I will never doubt the ability of educators to justify anything. The SETF pointed out that teaching assistants teach students during lunch and recess in order to justify the position. They appeared to be less concerned by the fact that teaching assistants are used as substitutes for other classes in the district and are left alone in their classroom when their special education teachers at-

CHART 10.1 Teaching Assistants' Time on Task.

	Time for Two Weeks (in minutes)	Percent of Times
General subjects	254.8	7.0%
Individual instruction	464.6	12.8%
Small-group instruction	466.6	12.9%
Large-group instruction	496.7	13.7%
Behavior	201.6	5.5%
Administrative work	349.9	9.6%
Substituting	288.8	7.9%
Lunch, dismissal duty		
Prep and recess	1090.3	30.1%
	3613.3	99.5%

tend meetings. This situation raises questions of the integrity of this program and the need for the teaching assistants.

STEPS FOR DIRECTORS OF SPECIAL EDUCATION TO TAKE TO IMPROVE THE SUPERVISION OF SPECIAL EDUCATION TEACHING ASSISTANTS

The first step to take to improve the supervision of special education teaching assistants is to spell out the role and tasks of teaching assistants. The second step is for special education teachers to spell out in their planbooks how teaching assistants will be used each day. The third step is for the director of special education to formally observe the use of teaching assistants in the classrooms, the fourth step is to have teaching assistants map their time on task weekly.

PSYCHOLOGISTS, SOCIAL WORKERS, AND LEARNING DISABILITIES TEACHER-CONSULTANTS

In district after district, I hear directors of special education moan and groan that psychologists are overworked and that the directors need more psychologists. In one district, the superintendent was concerned by the inability of the special education department in a county high school to meet state time lines for the evaluation of students. The district decided to find out what psychologists, social workers, and LD teacher-consultants did at work.

For twenty-seven weeks I used the curriculum mapping software CMT: FOR TEACHERS to determine patterns of activities of psychologists, social workers, and LD teacher-consultants in the high school and the time they spent on fifty-one tasks, divided into five areas, i.e., the application process, annual reviews, triennial reviews, new referrals, and miscellaneous activities. The application process includes such tasks as writing admission reports, correspondence with the student's home school, writing instructional guides, parent meet-

ings, team consultants, and meetings. Miscellaneous activities covered anything that did not relate to the application process, annual or triennial reviews, or new referrals. This includes such tasks as providing counseling, team consultations/meetings, telephone calls, visiting students' homes, writing state and federal reports, and inservice training.

As you can see from Chart 10.2, the lion's share of time was spent on miscellaneous activities, that is, activities that do not relate directly to special education. However, more detailed analysis of the detailed data indicated that these people could not account for approximately 20% of time that they should have been working; they worked twenty-six hours a week. There was a great deal of duplication of tasks by psychologists, social workers, and LD teachers-consultants in the high school. The audit indicated that the LD teacher-consultant spent twenty-five hours on home visits. Psychologists did not make any classroom observations. LD teacher-consultants and social workers spent a total of forty-five minutes observing new referrals in classrooms.

Curriculum mapping data helped to provide baseline data to determine time requirements to complete each task. In order to determine the time needed to complete serial tasks, a common unit of time measure was used and labeled "combined time." "Combined time" equaled all time spent on a task by all members of the team involved with the task. This information helped me to determine the time requirements to complete all incomplete tasks and to monitor the ability of special education to comply with all federal, state, and local time lines. With the data I gathered, I was able to determine that, on the average, it took

- 1.2 hours to screen a student
- 1.7 hours to complete an IEP
- 3.5 hours to complete an annual review
- 26 hours to process each new referral

Findings from this audit raised at least three questions:

CHART 10.2 Emphasis Each Position Placed on Each Area, i.e., Application Process, Annual and Triennial Reviews, New Referrals, and Miscellaneous Activities.

| | Position | | |
Area	Psychologist	Social Worker	LD Teacher-Consultant
Application process	9	3	5
Annual review	21	5	16
Triennial review	10	8	17
New referrals	17	30	11
Miscellaneous activities	43	53	51

(1) Is it appropriate for an LD teacher-consultant to spend twenty-five hours on home visits? What are the appropriate tasks for each position?

(2) Is it reasonable to spend twenty-six hours to process each new referral? What does it cost to process each new referral in your district?

(3) Should psychologists make classroom observations of students and teachers?

STEPS FOR DIRECTORS OF SPECIAL EDUCATION TO TAKE TO IMPROVE THE SUPERVISION OF PSYCHOLOGISTS, SOCIAL WORKERS, AND LD TEACHER-CONSULTANTS

The first step you need to take is to have your director of special education spell out the tasks of the psychologists, social workers, and LD teacher-consultants and the approximate amount of time required to perform each task. With this information, you can calculate the cost of each task. The second step that your director of special education needs to take is to determine the time parameters needed for a task to be completed by more than one position. And the third step to improve the supervision, effectiveness, and efficiency of special education support personnel is to determine if there are sufficient personnel to carry out the required tasks. Once you know the amount of time required to carry out each task, you can calculate the amount of personnel needed to complete all evaluations and annual and triennial reviews in a timely fashion.

SUMMARY

This chapter has explained to you the steps you need to take to improve the supervision of special education teachers and the efficiency and cost-effectiveness of teaching assistants, psychologists, social workers, and LD teacher-consultants. There is little doubt that there is a need in some districts, perhaps your own, to improve the supervision of special education teachers. You now know the specific steps you need to take to use the director of special education, principals, and chairpersons more effectively and efficiently to observe and evaluate special education teachers, review their planbooks, and provide advice to them. More importantly, you know how to make the director of special education more useful to your district. Your director of special education is able to assure members of the board of education and the superintendent of schools that the money for teaching assistants, psychologists, social workers, and LD teacher-consultants is well spent.

11

Supervision of the Special Education Curriculum

AIM

ALL too often, I have found that directors of special education give little attention to the curriculum taught to special education students. Sometimes, they do not know whether they have a curriculum guide in place. More of the time, they do not know whether the special education curriculum corresponds to the general education curriculum, and they never know the degree to which the curriculum taught by special education teachers is aligned to the general education curriculum taught. In other words, directors of special education, at times, neglect an important, if not one of the most important, supervisory responsibility. The net effect of this neglect, or oversight, is surely that the special education program is not as effective and efficient in helping students move into the general education program. This chapter spells out two steps that you as an administrator/supervisor can take to align the special education curriculum with the general education curriculum. The curriculum audit process and curriculum mapping process and software (CMT: FOR TEACHERS) allow you and your special education teachers to, first, put in place a customized curriculum guide that reflects the learning styles and individual needs of special education students and yet emphasizes areas stressed in general education curriculum. There are explanations and charts to help you implement an audit of your curriculum, and illustrations that clarify likely results of a curriculum audit, specifically of social studies programs. The curriculum mapping process and software allows you to determine the degree to which instruction in special education programs corresponds to instruction in general classes. There are explanations and charts to help you implement a curriculum mapping project. You will see the benefits of such a project for you as a supervisor, for your teachers, and of course, for the students that you want to have the prerequisite cognitive, affective, and psychomotor content/skills/be-

haviors to function comfortably in a general education program.

INTRODUCTION

You need to know whether special education students have learned the cognitive, affective, and psychomotor content/skills/behaviors needed to be successful in general education programs. You need to know the degree of alignment between the special education curriculum objectives/IEP objectives and the objectives of the general program. You need to know the degree to which the breadth and depth of the general program is matched by the special education program. You need to know the degree to which the curriculum delivered to special education students is aligned with the curriculum delivered to students in general programs. The purpose of this chapter is to show you the steps to take to gather information about the special education curriculum in place and the special education program delivered to students. This is essential if you and/or your director of special education is to be an effective and efficient administrator/supervisor.

Let me tell you up front that you need to be concerned about the special education curriculum because, in all my special education audits, I have found substantial gaps between the general curriculum and the special education curriculum. In my audits, I have shown that, based on programs of study, special education students in self-contained classes have not learned the body of prerequisite information expected of students in general classes. There is limited linkage between special education curriculum and general curriculum. You need to be able to establish linkage between special education curriculum and general curriculum in order to ensure special education students and their parents that the special education program is more than a holding area or babysitting area. You need to convince them that the special education curriculum permits a student to move comfortably into the mainstream program.

In order to determine the congruency between these special education and general programs, I have conducted curriculum audits and curriculum mapping programs. The audits are to determine whether the curriculum is in place. It is a paper audit. The curriculum mapping projects determine to what degree the program has been taught. The New York State Education Department has told all members of boards of education, superintendents, principals, and teachers in the state that

> The majority of students with disabilities have the intellectual potential to master the curricula content requirements for a high school diploma. . . . It is very important that at all grade levels students with handicapping conditions receive instruction in the same content areas so as to receive the same informational base that will be required for proficiency on statewide testing programs and diploma requirements.

SOCIAL STUDIES AUDITS

In order for you to determine whether special education youngsters learn the same content areas as the general program and whether the special education curriculum encompasses the same breadth and depth of content area as the general program, it is necessary to implement a curriculum audit. By the way, the information you gather through a curriculum audit helps special education teachers strengthen their programs. Specifically, the audit provides quantified information as to the number of times social studies or English or mathematics goals are written into the special education social studies, English, or mathematics IEP objectives and/or course objectives. For example, one district's social studies goal is for students to "participate as informed citizens in the political and economic systems of the United States." Based on the terms and phrases found in the IEP and special education social studies course objectives for a district, a customized list of terms and phrases is created to provide an operational definition for each goal. In this case, twelve terms/phrases are used as operational definitions for the goal. Any time these terms/phrases appeared in the IEP or special education social studies objectives, it counted as one occurrence of the district goal. The twelve terms used to define the goal "participate as informed citizens in the political and economic systems of the United States" are

(1) Attitude toward our national symbols
(2) Standing posture for the Pledge of Allegiance

(3) Knowing the American Flag has three colors
(4) Decisions about money
(5) Structure of the United States government
(6) Nation's symbols
(7) Awareness of specialization of labor and trade necessary to meet our needs
(8) Exchange of labor for capital
(9) Communities dependent on taxes
(10) Locations and boundaries
(11) Need for planning in political action to effect change
(12) Whether we can influence our taxes

As a result of this process, I am able to determine that the secondary special education social studies objectives in one district allocated 5% of the curriculum to information that would allow students to "participate as informed citizens in the political and economic systems of the United States." In the worst case scenario, you are able to identify goals/objectives that are not included in the special education curriculum objectives/IEP objectives. Chart 11.1 identifies the emphasis placed on each district social studies goal/objective in the special education program in descending order. You can determine whether you want your program to put greater, the same, or less emphasis on a particular goal/objective.

With this curriculum audit process, it is possible to better determine the degree to which linkage exists between national, state, and/or district goals/objectives and the social studies program in place for your special education program. In virtually every audit that I implemented, directors of special education, principals, and special education teachers point out that special education teachers either followed the state syllabi and/or the social studies curriculum in place in the district for the general classes. In most cases, directors of special education are confident that there is a high degree of linkage between the state social studies syllabi/district social studies general curriculum and the special education social studies curriculum guides. Unfortunately, the facts do not bear out their perceptions. My audits indicate that there is limited linkage between special education and general education curriculum. In the first instance, many districts lack a special education curriculum guide, one that spells out the goals, measurable objectives, content/skills, activities, resources, and evaluation method. In the second instance, districts that have portions of a special education curriculum guide in place do not place the same emphasis on the goals/objectives as placed in the general curriculum. In the worst scenario, supervisory personnel just do not care about the special education curriculum.

CHART 11.1 Emphasis Placed on Each District Social Studies Goal in the Special Education Program in Descending Order.

District Social Studies Goals	Emphasis Placed on Goals in Special Education IEP/Social Studies Objectives (%)
1. Communicate information clearly and effectively in both oral and written form.	14
2. Explain the historic, economic, social, and political roots of major cultures of the world.	12
3. Describe and analyze major historic factors in the development of the United States.	10
4. Discuss the nature and effects of change on societies and individuals.	6
5. Explain how societies teach individuals to live within specific values systems.	6
6. Describe the results of the interactions between individuals and societies and the environment.	6
7. Organize, analyze, and interpret information in all forms.	6
8. Empathize with the values that guide the behavior of people from different cultures.	5
9. Gather information by listening, reading, and observing with accuracy and comprehension.	5
10. Identify important social studies ideas and methodologies and apply them to new information and experiences.	5
11. Participate as informed citizens in the political and economic systems of the United States.	5
12. Analyze the effects of geography on the development of cultures.	5
13. Explain the fundamental similarities and differences among major economic, social, and political systems and how these systems operate in an interdependent world.	4
14. Use the vocabulary of social studies in appropriate context.	3
15. Demonstrate knowledge of the increasing international connections of social and political systems and how these systems operate in an interdependent world.	2
16. Value the principles and ideals of a democratic system based upon the premise of human dignity, liberty, justice, and equality.	2
17. Compare the rights and responsibilities of citizens of the United States with the rights and responsibilities of citizens of other societies.	1
18. Demonstrate the skills that enable people to participate reasonably in a democratic society.	1
19. Demonstrate an enhanced perspective of self as one who benefits from the human experience and who participates in and contributes to that experience.	1
20. Explain the relationship between social studies learning and learning that takes place in other disciplines and other institutions.	0

SOCIAL STUDIES UNDERSTANDINGS/OBJECTIVES

In order to explain to you the steps in the special education curriculum audit process, I need to walk you through a curriculum, in this case, the New York State syllabi used in general social studies classes. In order for you to identify some problems that you are likely to encounter in your own audit, I have included examples from three districts, Districts 3, 4, and 5.

You need to identify the number of different goals, objectives, understandings, or concepts in the general curriculum. New York State syllabi identify social studies understandings and/or objectives for each grade. The number of social studies understandings and/or objectives by grade are

Grade	Number of Understandings and/or Objectives
1	29
2	28
3	24
4	30
5	26
6	36
7 and 8	46
9 and 10	214

The questions that you need to wrestle with are how many of the understandings/objectives are included in the special education social studies objectives/IEP objectives, and how do you gather this information. The illustrations from Districts 3 and 4 explain the methods and different processes to use to conduct a curriculum audit.

ILLUSTRATION FROM DISTRICT 3

This illustration is used to show you how to conduct an audit when the district lacks a special education social studies curriculum guide. First, you need to determine whether the district's special education social studies curriculum has all the components of a curriculum guide. In District 3, the elementary special education social studies program lacks any formal curriculum guides that spell out goals, objectives, content, skills, activities/strategies/methods, resources, and evaluation. However, there are some items in place. Grade level teachers cite specific textbooks as their curriculum guides and include a copy of the scope and sequence from the textbooks. In most cases, special education teachers have developed individual units for the program, but oftentimes, these units spell out concepts, content, and/or stories to read. Sometimes, special education teachers cite supplementary materials.

The secondary special education social studies program lacks any formal curriculum guide; however, one secondary special education teacher did submit a copy of a guide used in general classes. This guide identifies content and time lines but does not include information regarding resources, activities, strategies, or methods. Another special education teacher did submit a guide with a philosophy statement, and two people did submit copies of the state syllabi.

I have four concerns about the special education social studies program in this district. First, I want to know why the director of special education and/or the assistant superintendent of curriculum and instruction did not monitor the special education curriculum and take steps to make sure an organic curriculum was in place for special education students. Second, there is not a formal customized special education social studies curriculum guide in place. The curriculum guide should contain the goals/measurable objectives, content, skills, activities, resources, evaluation method, and time parameters for the delivery of each objective. Third, there is not any document in place to indicate that there is either horizontal or vertical articulation of the program. Fourth, there is no way to establish linkage between the depth and breadth of the special education social studies program and state syllabi and/or general district social studies program because there is no special education social studies curriculum in place. Ultimately, the question asked is, who is minding the special education program?

ILLUSTRATION FROM DISTRICT 4

In District 4, a curriculum audit was conducted to determine the degree to which linkage existed between the social studies syllabi and the special education IEP social studies objectives. In grades 1–6, each IEP social studies objective for a grade level is linked to a syllabus understanding. In grades 7–12, each IEP social studies objective for a grade level is linked to a

CHART 11.2 Degree of Linkage between IEP Social Studies Objectives and the State Syllabi Understandings and Objectives.

Grades	Degree of Linkage (%)
1	45
2	61
3	88
4	73
5	96
6	94
7/8	63
9/10	56
11	36
12 (Economics)	47

syllabus objective. Some IEP social studies objectives include more than one of the understandings or objectives in a syllabus.

The curriculum audit indicates a number of problems with the special education social studies program, especially at the secondary level. Material is outdated. The tenth-grade IEP objectives relate to local history when, in fact, the present tenth-grade program deals with global studies. The IEP objectives for the ninth and tenth grades virtually omit Latin America. The IEP objectives, grades 1–12, are not grouped into categories found in the New York State syllabi under understandings and objectives. Some IEP objectives are broad and vague.

Chart 11.2 indicates that there is a greater degree of linkage between the IEP social studies objectives and the state syllabi understandings and objectives in grades 5 and 6 and a lesser degree of linkage in grades 7–12.

ILLUSTRATIONS FROM DISTRICT 5

Let this information from District 5 serve as a warning to you to be skeptical when anyone tells you that the special education curriculum is equal to the general program. You might shudder at the findings from District 5 the way I do every time I review my audit of that district. First, 63% of teachers in the special education program report that there is no formal horizontal and vertical articulation of programs. Second, three out of four chairpersons are not aware of any formal and vertical articulation of programs. Four out of six principals and three out of four chairpersons do not know how the special education program is supervised to insure that IEP objectives are achieved, and one chairperson notes that he/she is not motivated to learn about special education because it requires specialized training. With this type of administrative/supervisory commitment to the education of all students, is there any wonder why some people believe that special education is an ineffective program, merely a public babysitting service that expects and gets little from students in the program?

In District 5, each high school special education class is taught by a content teacher and a special education teacher. Subject teachers and special education teachers in the special education program point out that, in regards to syllabuses and curriculum,

Subject Teacher	Special Education Teacher
• The state syllabus was used but not in depth. • There was no printed syllabus. • We modified the general level curriculum. • We watered down the general program. • We are still setting up curriculum. • There weren't any course objectives.	• not sure where curriculum comes from • general level curriculum broken down differently with a special education presentation • never saw curriculum and never went over it with subject leader • wrote my own curriculum, which is different from the general program

Subject teachers and special education teachers in the special education program pointed out that, in regards to IEPs

Subject Teacher	Special Education Teacher
• read through IEPs • have not seen IEP objectives • have never had access to files and do not know what are the students' disabilities	• general social studies goals • blanket IEP for earth science • IEP not gone over by content teacher

What I found most interesting was that 78% of high school classroom teachers knew in their heart of hearts that the special education curriculum was not equal to the general program. What I found unforgivable was that three out of four subject chairpersons had not read the special education curriculum and did not know the degree of linkage between the special education document and the general program, much less the state syllabus, even though they had supervisory responsibilities for the special education classes in their subject area. And, finally, only four out of eighteen special

education classes were observed by either the principals, the director of special education, or the chairpersons.

STEPS YOU CAN TAKE TO IMPROVE YOUR SPECIAL EDUCATION CURRICULUM

In order to strengthen your special education curriculum, you need first to hold the director of special education responsible for special education curriculum. In all likelihood, the director of special education will need to increase his/her knowledge of curriculum design, planning, implementation, and evaluation. Second, you need to make sure your curriculum guides identify goals, measurable objectives, content, skills, activities, resources, and evaluation methods. Third, you need to determine the degree of linkage between the goals, objectives, understandings, or concepts found in the special education and general curriculum. Fourth, determine whether you need to change the emphasis placed on specific goals, objectives, concepts, or understandings. If you take these steps, you will have in place a curriculum guide that, if implemented by special education teachers and learned by special education students, will help students to move into a general program.

CURRICULUM MAPPING

Once you have put a curriculum in place, you need to determine the degree to which it is taught to students. Curriculum mapping is a procedure by which administrators and teachers can monitor the allocation of classroom time in order to ensure that standards, goals, and/or measurable objectives are met consistently. In this process, each teacher maintains a log, or map. The teacher records the classroom time, in minutes, that either an entire class or an individual student actually spent on each of a number of standards, goals, objectives, subjects, topics, content, skills, or behaviors. These data are entered into a software program (CMT: FOR TEACHERS), which generates individual teacher and student reports and horizontal and vertical articulation grade reports.

I have designed, planned, and implemented curriculum mapping programs in order to determine the degree to which special education teachers instructed students in the areas taught in the general classes. In addition, CMT: FOR TEACHERS has been used to determine how administrators, psychologists, and social workers use their time.

CHART 11.3 The Average Amount of Instructional Time (in minutes) Spent by 110 Teachers in Grades PK, K, 1, 2, 3, SE 1–3, 4, 5, 6, SE 4–6 on Eleven Health Education Concepts.

	Grades									
	PK	K	1	2	3	SE 1–3	4	5	6	SE 4–6
Human growth and development	518	719	291	319	304	218	78	262	344	399
Emotional health	378	599	376	534	1195	229	264	334	1016	1280
Nutrition	704	481	361	395	195	327	56	168	208	223
Environmental health	125	299	188	191	296	100	139	220	409	418
Family life education	130	362	157	123	151	169	18	41	162	214
Diseases and disorders	237	298	164	107	94	96	59	71	385	341
Consumer health	23	45	66	32	29	26	9	12	145	79
Alcohol, tobacco, and other drug substances	75	57	141	237	141	111	88	257	903	458
Safety, first aid, and survival	312	469	350	465	367	65	68	169	303	263
Community health	30	122	37	45	16	21	12	8	151	16
Healthful lifestyles	288	413	210	265	264	160	59	68	479	318
Total	2820	3864	2341	2713	3052	1522	852	1610	4503	4007

ILLUSTRATION: ALIGNMENT BETWEEN GENERAL HEALTH PROGRAM AND THE SPECIAL EDUCATION HEALTH PROGRAM BY GRADE LEVEL

I think you will find one of my curriculum mapping projects enlightening. The project was to gather data on the delivery of the elementary health education program in four districts by 110 teachers, including seven special education teachers. The goals for this program were to gather data on the total and average time spent on the eleven concepts, thirty-four objectives, and 108 learning outcomes in the health syllabus by class, grade, and district. As a result of these data I was able to determine the degree of linkage between the health curriculum delivered to general and special education students.

Chart 11.3 indicates that the one area that special education students, grades 1–6, spent more time learning about than the students in general programs, grade 1–6, was family life education. The objectives for family life education were for students to

- appreciate the role of the family in society
- demonstrate an understanding of human sexuality
- understand the responsibility of the family in providing a foundation for the health of succeeding generations

Also, students in special education, grades 4–6, spent more time learning about human growth and development, emotional health, nutrition, and environmental health than students in general classes, grades 4–6.

You must wonder, as I do, why special education teachers spend more time on family life education than teachers in general classes. Why is there an increased emphasis on health education for special education students in grades 4–6?

CHART 11.4 Percent of Instructional Time Special Education Students Spent on Concepts, Topics, Content, and Skills (in and out) of the General Curriculum by Grade.

Grades	English		Social Studies		Science		Mathematics	
	In	Out	In	Out	In	Out	In	Out
7	93	7	90	10	92	8	100	0
8	96	4	87	13	91	9	100	0
9	86	14	94	6	100	0	98	2
10	98	2	99	1	81	19	0	100
11	98	2	99	1	45	55	0	0

ILLUSTRATION: ALIGNMENT BETWEEN GENERAL HIGH SCHOOL ENGLISH, SOCIAL STUDIES, SCIENCE, AND MATHEMATICS PROGRAMS AND THE SPECIAL EDUCATION PROGRAMS

In one district, I had special education teachers map time that randomly selected students spent on English, social studies, science, and mathematics. Not all the students spent time on each of the subject areas; However, Chart 11.4 indicates the percent of time that was spent on concepts, topics, content, and skills in and out of the general curriculum by these selected students, grades 7–11. As you can see, notable changes in program delivery take place in grades 10 and 11. The English and social studies programs mirror the general curriculum, while the science and mathematics programs differ from the general curriculum.

PARENTS

You will find that, generally, the parents of special education youngsters have positive comments about the subjects their children study. In one district, parents of a high school student wrote, ''We feel that the special education program has provided our child with a good academic program and caring teachers. The program is structured and well run.'' However, some of the parents were less than positive about the courses studied, and based on findings from my curriculum audits and curriculum mapping projects, some of these parents were very perceptive. Without overstating the comments of the few parents, you need to know that they were concerned about the breadth and depth of courses for their children. They either felt that there was a need for more computers or thought that the program was not challenging enough or doubted that the program was aligned to the general curriculum. Here are sample comments made by parents:

- I think greater emphasis should be put on seeing that homework and classwork are completed. Teachers should have students stay after school to reinforce study habits.
- Subjects don't follow third grade curriculum—no books—all I see is art work.
- At the present time, the subjects are behind two years.

- At the senior level, the curriculum is too simplistic.
- The curriculum is not indepth enough.

SUMMARY

In order to strengthen your special education curriculum, you need to first make sure that the goals, objectives, content, skills, and behaviors taught in special education classes were those that were spelled out in the curriculum guides. Second, you need to determine the degree to which the delivered curriculum in special education corresponds to the curriculum taught in general education programs, and you can best accomplish this by use of a curriculum mapping program, i.e., CMT: FOR TEACHERS. With the information gathered by curriculum mapping, you and your teachers can modify the special education program so that it is better aligned with the general education program delivered to students. Once again, this process helps students learn materials that they need if they are to make a successful transition into a general education class.

You now know of two steps that you can take to become a more effective supervisor and improve the special education curriculum. This chapter spells out two steps that you as an administrator/supervisor can take to align the special education curriculum with the general education curriculum. The curriculum audit process and curriculum mapping software (CMT: FOR TEACHERS) allows you and your special education teachers to, first, put in place a customized curriculum guide that reflects the learning styles and individual needs of special education students and yet emphasizes areas stressed in general education curriculum. There are explanations and charts to help you implement a curriculum audit of your curriculum and illustrations that clarify likely results of a curriculum audit, specifically of social studies programs. The curriculum mapping process and software allows you to determine the degree to which instruction in special education programs corresponds to instruction in general classes. There are explanations and charts to help you implement curriculum mapping projects and see the benefits of such a program for you as a supervisor, for your teachers, and of course, for students that you want to be able to have the prerequisite cognitive, affective, and psychomotor content/skills/behaviors to function comfortably in a general education program.

12

Accountability of Special Education Programs: Length of Time Students Are Classified, Pull-Out Programs, and Placement of Minority Students

AIM

THIS chapter walks you through a process that helps you downsize your special education program ethically and methodically and, at all times, maintains the integrity of the special education program for students who need to be classified. First, you are walked through the steps you need to take to determine the average length of time that an average classified student is classified by category. You are led into the area of accountability where none exists in special education. Namely, you and your special education staff need to explain why it takes more than five years to get either an LD, SI, or ED student back into general classes. Second, you are asked to question the benefits of pull-out programs for LD, SI, and ED students and to calculate the financial costs of pull-out programs. Would students in pull-out programs benefit more from remaining all day in their general classes, perhaps with consultants? Are your staff and money used effectively and efficiently in pull-out programs? Would your staff and money be used more effectively and efficiently if pull-out students remained in their general classes for all instruction? Third, you are walked through steps to determine whether ethnicity/race is a factor in the placement of students within the LD, SI, and ED categories. Each of these steps touches on equity issues, program accountability, and educational issues. Ultimately, they influence the size and cost of special education. This chapter helps you to downsize special education and reduce costs in a methodical manner if you find that there is fat in your special education program.

INTRODUCTION

You probably have an accurate perception of the makeup of students in your special education program, and it probably is similar to findings such as those in my special education audits. My special education audits indicate that students classified LD, SI, and ED account for over 85% of the special education population, and students classified LD make up anywhere from 53% to 64% of youngsters in special education. The lion's share of these students is males. Males make up approximately 66% of classified students, and your special education minority population is proportionally greater than minority enrollment in your district. But there is much more that you need to know about your special education program if you want to operate an equitable, objective, and effective special education program.

This chapter walks you through a five-step process that builds accountability into your special education program and explains subtleties that affect the equity, objectivity, and effectiveness of your program. You need to know the length of time students are classified by ethnicity/race and by category in your school/district. You need to calculate the cost of pull-out programs, and you need to know the subtleties that ethnicity/race play in the placement of classified students by categories. These three issues are center to any discussion of the size and cost of special education. Also, they are at the heart of any discussion related to public confidence in the special education program. The five steps spelled out in this chapter will help you develop greater program accountability and a more effective and efficient special education program.

FIRST STEP TO DOWNSIZE THE NUMBER OF CLASSIFIED STUDENTS BY CATEGORIES

The first step to downsize the number of classified students and yet maintain the educational integrity of special education is to find out the number of students classified by category in your district. The purpose of Chart 12.1 is to show you that, regardless of the size of your district, you can expect to find the bulk of students classified LD, SI, ED, and OHI. And you need to know

CHART 12.1 The Number of Students Classified by Category for Districts 6 and 7.

Classification	District 6, Total Number	District 7, Total Number
LD	1244	294
SI	503	73
ED	293	31
OHI	143	10
MH	92	6
MR	63	1
HH	30	2
DE	15	1
OI	15	7
AUT	9	0
VI	5	0
	2412	425

that it is possible that you will not have students in all categories. This information helps you to identify the emphasis of your special education program and raise at least four questions about the size of each category of students. For instance, what are the reasons for so many students being classified LD? How does the number and percent of students classified SI compare with the figures nationally, statewide, and countywide? And more importantly, why are the youngsters in your district classified SI? How many months does a student remain classified by category? The answers to these three questions impact on the size and cost of your special education program.

SECOND STEP TO DOWNSIZE THE NUMBER OF CLASSIFIED STUDENTS BY CATEGORIES

The second step to downsize the number of classified students and and yet maintain the educational integrity

of special education is to find out the length of time students are classified by categories. As you can see, Chart 12.2 indicates that students are classified, on the average, anywhere from sixteen months to eighty-six months, depending on their handicapping conditions. The average length of time students are classified LD, SI, and ED is rather consistent from district to district; however, there is less consistency in other classifications from Districts 6 and 7. Although you can understand the fact that students who are deaf, autistic, and visually impaired will remain classified for their entire school experience, you probably have questions about the reasons for LD students remaining classified for about four years. After all, these students make up the lion's share of classified students, and if you can reduce the length of time the average student remains classified, you can reduce the costs of the special education program. You have identified the problem; now you have to find a solution that ensures that students who are truly LD and need special education services

CHART 12.2 Average Number of Months That a Student Is Classified by Category.

Classification	District 6, Average Length of Time (in months) Classified	District 7, Average Length of Time (in months) Classified
DE	80	0
MR	76	20
HH	64	16
MH	57	20
LD	55	47
AUT	52	0
OI	47	86
VI	43	0
ED	39	25
OHI	38	64
SI	31	31
HI	0	76

receive special education services but that students who can function well without special education services are declassified.

THIRD STEP TO DOWNSIZE THE NUMBER OF CLASSIFIED STUDENTS BY CATEGORIES

The third step to downsize the number of classified students and yet maintain the educational integrity of special education is to find out the length of time students are classified by grade level. When you review Chart 12.3, you have to wonder whether special education programs truly help students develop the learning skills and behaviors that allow them to compensate for their disabilities and return to the general program. After all, in Districts 6 and 7, the longer students are in school, the longer they remain classified. If you are to make the special education program accountable and understandable to members of the board of education and the entire school community, then you and they both need to know the length of time students have been classified by category by grade. You and they need to know the percent of classified students that are in self-contained classes and the percent of students that receive regular classroom instruction and related services or resource room or part-time special class programs. This information provides you and them with a more realistic picture of the extent of services received by each student.

FOURTH STEP TO DOWNSIZE THE NUMBER OF CLASSIFIED STUDENTS BY CATEGORIES

The fourth step to downsize the number of classified students and and yet maintain the educational integrity of special education is to analyze the length of time

students are classified by category by grade level, the number of full-time equivalent (FTE) teachers for each program, and the number of students who receive regular classroom instruction and related services or resource room or part-time special class programs. You need to look at students classified LD, SI, and ED specifically if you want to make a dent in downsizing special education.

MAINSTREAMING

Before I discuss the LD, SI, and ED programs in greater depth, I need to share my perceptions and findings with you about the mainstreaming process. You and I use the term *mainstreaming*. Governmental agencies talk about students who receive regular classroom instruction and related services or resource room or part-time special class programs.

When you speak with special education personnel, you come away with the feeling that they are fed up with the picture that exists of special education as a black hole, a place where youngsters are swallowed up never to be heard from again by general education teachers. Well, nothing is further from the truth. You will see that over half the children classified SI, approximately a third of youngsters classified LD, and a fifth of students classified ED receive regular classroom instruction and related services or resource room or part-time special class programs. In other words, a substantial portion of classified youngsters are mainstreamed for part of their education. And this is probably the situation in your school/district.

Now that you understand that a good number of these youngsters resurface in general classes, you need to know if there is a systematic process in place in your school/district to determine which students should be mainstreamed and in which classes. Does the process allow you to determine, with some certainty, that

CHART 12.3 The Average Length of Time (by grade by months) That Students Were Classified.

Grade	District 6, Number of Months	District 7, Number of Months
1	21.3	27.8
2	29.2	23.7
3	31.5	34.3
4	35.3	32.3
5	39.5	42.6
6	45.5	48.0
7	55.0	54.2
8	61.6	66.1
9	62.4	77.5
10	70.0	62.3
11	75.4	64.0
12	84.6	70.5

mainstreamed students have a reasonable chance of success in general education classes? Are you assured that all students who should be mainstreamed are mainstreamed? Unfortunately, you will be depressed by the "fly by the seat of your pants" operation to mainstream students, yet there are procedures and instruments in place in most schools/districts that could easily be used as the foundation for a systematic process for mainstreaming students.

CRITERIA USED TO MAINSTREAM STUDENTS

If your school/district is anything like the schools/districts I audited, then you probably do not have any specific district criteria, written or unwritten, to mainstream students. Sometimes, I have the feeling that, when a special education teacher has a student that he/she thinks should be mainstreamed, the special education teacher roams the halls of his/her school to snatch a general education teacher willing to permit a classified student in class. Normally, the special education teacher tells the general education teacher that the general education teacher is good with students, is really sensitive to the needs of students, and is the only teacher that could work effectively with the youngster to be mainstreamed. Most of the time, it seems that this is a black market operation out of the sight of administrators/supervisors or a cottage industry. It has all the tones of a speakeasy operation, and the special education teacher has to say those magic words, "Please help me; no one else will give the youngster a chance." As one special education teacher lamented, "The criteria are set, unfortunately, by teachers receiv-

ing students or by department classification. There are no firm criteria." And that is truly unfortunate and unfair to classified students.

You can expect to find that all buildings in your district have their own method for mainstreaming students, a thought that does not inspire you to believe that the mainstreaming process is equitable, objective, or effective. Yet special education teachers, principals, and CSE members from different districts report some common procedures and common instruments used to decide whether a student should be mainstreamed. Also, they point out the areas most often cited as considerations for mainstreaming students, such as academic performance, age appropriate behavior, strong study and/or subject area skills, ability to function with minimal or no special education intervention, student's internal motivation, and teacher evaluation.

LEARNING DISABLED

Because the bulk of students in your district are classified LD, it is reasonable for you to take a closer look at LD program to see if there is unnecessary fat in the program. Districts 6 and 7 differ in size and in demographics; however, they both have a similar percent of LD students that have been in the program less than and more than five years. Charts 12.4A and 12.4B indicate that between 61% and 66% of LD students have been classified for less than five years. These charts indicate that between 34% and 39% of students were classified for more than five years. You need to know why a third of LD students have been classified

CHART 12.4A The Number of Months Students in District 6 Had Been Classified Learning Disabled as of 1993–1994 (by grade by number of students).

	Number of Months														
Grade	12	24	36	48	60	72	84	96	108	120	132	144	156	168	Total
K	13	5	0	1											19
1	12	19	10	3	3										47
2	21	22	19	17	9	3									91
3	17	19	28	20	11	4									99
4	18	18	21	23	11	14	3	1							109
5	11	12	21	24	15	10	7	2							102
6	11	15	16	21	15	8	18	7	1						112
7	7	5	11	10	16	17	15	7	5	3					96
8	7	5	8	21	17	14	22	21	13	3	2	1	0	1	135
9	8	7	10	12	8	12	12	11	10	10	4	3			107
10	2	3	7	4	10	10	6	7	9	7	6	2	5		78
11	8	5	5	5	6	5	8	7	13	12	11	4	2		91
12	2	4	2	0	3	4	10	16	13	15	8	5	8		90
	137	139	158	161	124	101	101	79	64	50	31	15	15	1	1176

Chart indicates that thirteen kindergarten students spent between one and twelve months classified learning disabled.

CHART 12.4B The Number of Months Students Had Been Classified Learning Disabled as of 1990–1991 (by grade by number of students).

Grade	Number of Months													Total
	12	24	36	48	60	72	84	96	108	120	132	144	156	
K	14													14
1	4	3	4	4										15
2	11	4	7	2	1									25
3	6	6	5	8	2	2								29
4	8	5	4	9	6	1								33
5	4	4	2	2	3	4	3	1						23
6	3	3	1	1	1	8	4	1	1					23
7	3	2	2	4	2	6	2	2	2					25
8	2	4	1	1	1	3	2	2	5	1				22
9	3	2	0	0	0	3	0	5	4	1	1			19
10	4	3	2	2	2	1	5	1	4	4	0			28
11	2	3	0	3	3	1	3	2	2	1	4	1		25
12	1	1	0	1	2	0	0	3	1	0	0	3	1	13
Total	65	40	28	37	23	29	19	17	19	7	5	4	1	294

Chart indicates that fourteen kindergarten students spent between one and twelve months classified learning disabled.

for more than five years. Is it reasonable to expect the LD program to develop the skills and behaviors in students that they need to be successful in general education programs within five years?

LENGTH OF TIME STUDENTS ARE CLASSIFIED LD BY ETHNICITY/RACE

One of the most interesting findings from my special education audit of District 6 is that white students tend to be classified LD for a longer period of time than Latino and African American students. Also, a larger percentage of white students spend five years or more classified LD than do Latino and African American students. Chart 12.5 indicates that, in District 6, the LD program tends to retain white students more than Latino and African American students.

INSIGHTS PROVIDED BY PSYCHOLOGISTS ABOUT THE LENGTH OF TIME THAT STUDENTS ARE CLASSIFIED LD

Psychologists shed some light on the question, ''Is it reasonable for a district to expect that mildly/moderately handicapped LD students will learn to compensate

for their learning disabilities in less than five years?'' In my audits, I found that they indicated that one need not be classified LD forever. They pointed out that, once one learned to compensate for the learning disability and services were no longer needed, one would be declassified.

There are subtle differences and some contradictory comments made by psychologists, special education teachers, and principals regarding the length of time students are classified LD. Some psychologists, special education teachers, and principals indicate that the reason learning disabled students spend a longer time in special education than emotionally disturbed students is because learning disabilities are neurologically and organically based. Because they are more difficult to remediate than emotionally disturbed problems, they require more time. Other psychologists, special education teachers, and principals point out that students can be declassified if they learn to compensate for their learning disabilities. Here are a range of comments that you can expect to hear from your psychologists, special education teachers, and principals:

- LD is neurologically based and cannot be ''cured.''

CHART 12.5 Number of Months Students in District 6 Are Classified LD (by ethnicity/race).

Ethnicity/Race	Average Number of Months	Percent of Students Classified LD at Least 60 Months	Percent of Students That Moved or Dropped out of School
White	56	41	5
Hispanic	43	29	7
African American	40	21	5

- LD is something you can't change, but you learn to compensate and learn strategies. Emotional handicaps can be remediated through therapy. Each student remains classified as long as they need the services.
- LD cannot be "cured" whereas the behavior of ED students can be changed as a result of medication, counseling, and behavior modification techniques.
- LD students are learning disabled for life (it doesn't disappear after high school). They may need academic support well into their college years. ED students may learn to cope with the issues impeding academic progress and reach success sooner.
- LD is an area that will affect a child for life whereas behavior can be successfully managed or modified through therapy.
- LD is a neurologically based disorder; changes in functioning take longer as time is needed to develop compensatory strategies.
- LD students suffer from neurological impairments that are unresolvable. They must be taught compensatory methods.
- LD issues are oft-times neurologically based. All the behavior strategies, emotional support, improved decision making, modeling, and counseling in the world won't "fix" the problem. With such interventions, however, ED students can be rid of the classification.
- LD is something you can't change, but you learn to compensate and learn strategies. Emotional handicaps can be remediated through therapy. Each student remains classified as long as he/she need the services.
- An ED student is not necessarily academically deficient. The emotional issue might be interfering with the child's functioning level. An LD student, when classified, is severely deficient in one or more academic areas. Certain weaknesses can be remediated, and compensatory techniques taught, but a learning disability is never cured.
- A learning disability is usually a lifelong condition for which students must learn to compensate. An emotional handicap can often be "overcome" through support services.
- LD is not curable. You learn to compensate for it hopefully, and you are declassified—if you don't need services. However, an LD is always an LD.
- LD students have continued difficulty as the mainstream requirements increase.
- ED students can get specific counseling to remediate problems. LD students may need

longer to develop compensatory skills for what will be lifelong problems.
- LD students are identified earlier than ED students because the handicap is noticed more easily and a larger percentage of ED students are sent outside the district.
- ED students are identified earlier than LD students. Even though students are unable to read and write by the sixth grade, they are not identified as LD until seventh or eighth grade. By that time, their LD inhibited them from being mainstreamed in secondary school.
- There were a high number of LD students in the resource room.

Based upon comments made by psychologists, special education teachers, and principals, you have an obligation to ask them to help you determine reasonable time expectations to remediate LD students and to teach LD students compensatory techniques. As a matter of fact, this information should be part of the student's file and used as an accountability index for the special education program. If they expect the special education program to require more than five years to remediate and teach compensatory techniques to a LD student, then they should inform you regarding the reasons for the needed time.

LD STUDENTS WHO RECEIVE REGULAR CLASSROOM INSTRUCTION AND RELATED SERVICES OR RESOURCE ROOM OR PART-TIME SPECIAL CLASS PROGRAMS

You are aware of the brouhaha surrounding the issue of inclusion in special education. I have no intention to philosophize about the merits and demerits of inclusion for all classified students. However, I have and you may have concerns about the pros and cons of pull-out programs such as speech therapy, remedial reading, LD resource room, and counseling. As part of your special education audit, you need to determine whether LD students in general classes who receive related services or resource room or part-time special class programs can be serviced equally well all day in general classes, especially if there is a consultant available for the youngster and/or the general classroom teacher. In other words, have these students been remediated and have they learned compensatory techniques sufficiently to function well in general classes all day, rather than for most of the day? And are some students able to function well in general classes with the assistance of a consultant? If so, you have a reasonable way to downsize special education and reduce costs while maintaining the integrity of the special education program.

PARENTS' VIEWS ON PULL-OUT PROGRAMS

You need to know that there are parents that are not pleased with pull-out programs. In one special education audit, parents complained that

- My son misses too much class time.
- Sometimes the test modifications set aside for him are not always carried out.
- My daughter has a visual LD, and she is not learning how to overcome it in resource room. The teacher reads to her when she doesn't understand things.
- I am concerned that my child is being pulled out of class (more than once), and I am concerned with missed work.
- I am not sure if he is getting everything he needs and is not missing regular classwork.

CONSULTANT MODELS

In New York State, the commissioner of education notes that there are many ways to provide services for a pupil with handicapping conditions who attends a regular education program on a full-time basis and/or to such pupil's regular education teachers. The Updated Part 200 Regulations of the Commissioner of Education (April 1992) defines two types of consultant teacher services.

(1) Direct consultant teacher services means specially designed individualized or group instruction provided by a certified special education teacher to a pupil with a handicapping condition to aid such pupil to benefit from the pupil's regular education program.

(2) Indirect consultant teacher services means consultation provided by a certified special education teacher to regular education teachers to assist them in adjusting the learning environment and/or modifying their instructional methods to meet the individual needs of a pupil with a handicapping condition who attends classes.

LD STUDENTS IN PULL-OUT PROGRAMS: AN EXAMPLE

The number of LD students in pull-out programs varies considerably. I have seen districts that had 54% of their students receive regular classroom instruction and related services or resource room or part-time special class programs. In one district, a head count of LD students in the program indicates that 106 out of 294 (36%) students classified learning disabled, grades K−12, received regular classroom instruction and re-

lated services or resource room or part-time special class programs. The number of students by grade was

Grade	Number of Students
K	0
1	0
2	11
3	9
4	16
5	10
6	3
7	7
8	12
9	4
10	18
11	11
12	13
	114

You need to know that the issue here is whether these students can be educated as well in general classes all day as in general class for most of the day and in pull-out programs for the rest of the day. If these students have been remediated and have learned compensatory techniques sufficiently to function well in general classes all day, rather than for most of the day, they should be declassified according to psychologists, special education teachers, and principals. If some of these students are able to function well in general classes all day with the assistance of a consultant, would it be better for them to remain in their general classes or to be in pull-out classes? The net effect of declassifying these students or using a consultant model for those students in need is to reduce the size of the LD program conservatively by 36%.

NUMBER OF LD TEACHERS

My special education audits of different districts indicate that your resource room teachers probably account for 45% of the time special education teachers spend with LD students. You understand that a reduction in the number of LD students means that you can reduce the number of resource room teachers or or that you can use these teachers in some more effective manner. Some of these resource room teachers can be used as consultants and serve a larger number of students and general education teachers than they did as resource room teachers. You can determine the degree to which you can downsize this portion of your LD program and the amount of money you are able to save and still deliver a quality special education program.

SPEECH IMPAIRED

In the course of my special education audits, I have analyzed districts that had between 13% and 21% of students classified SI. In the course of these audits, there were areas of the program that warranted closer investigation to ensure that the program was effective and efficient. However, at first glance, there is nothing wrong with the length of time students are classified SI. Although Districts 8 and 9 differ in size and demographics, the bulk of students in both districts had been classified SI for less than five years. Charts 12.6A and 12.6B indicate that between 88% and 96% of students classified speech impaired had been classified for less than five years. On the other hand, between 4% and 12% of students were classified for more than five years. Nevertheless, you need to know why this small percent of SI students has been classified for more than five years.

LENGTH OF TIME STUDENTS ARE CLASSIFIED SI BY ETHNICITY/RACE

Although the information on ethnicity/race of students classified SI from my special education audit of District 8 cannot be generalized, it does show you how to determine whether there might be subtle problems inherent in the SI program. Chart 12.8 indicates that Latino students tend to be classified SI for a longer period of time than white and African American students. Also, a larger percentage of Latino students

spend five years or more classified SI than do white and African American students. More importantly, Chart 12.7 indicates that had minority students not moved or dropped out of school at a higher rate than white students, minority students would have made up an even larger percentage of students classified SI.

SI STUDENTS WHO RECEIVE REGULAR CLASSROOM INSTRUCTION AND RELATED SERVICES OR RESOURCE ROOM OR PART-TIME SPECIAL CLASS PROGRAMS

In New York State, approximately 55% of students classified SI receive regular classroom instruction and related services (speech language therapy). In District 7, 93% of students classified SI receive speech language therapy. Students who receive this service are provided with two (2) half-hour sessions of therapy per week. They are mainstreamed for all other subjects. Sixty-seven elementary students receive speech language therapy. Two students who receive this service are not classified SI. Seven students who are classified SI are not listed as receiving this service. In District 6, there are 486 students classified SI, but speech services are provided to twice that number of students.

If these were your districts, you would have a series of questions. What are the reasons for the disproportionate percent of students in District 7 receiving regular classroom instruction and speech therapy? Why

CHART 12.6A The Number of Months Students in District 8 Had Been Classified Speech Impaired (by grade by number of students).

Grade	Number of Months													Total
	12	24	36	48	60	72	84	96	108	120	132	144	156	
PS	1	1												2
K	43	52	1	1										97
1	22	15	46	3	3									89
2	9	18	27	32	10									96
3	3	10	10	9	9	2								43
4	4	4	8	3	4	8	2							33
5	11	4	4	5	3	3	5							35
6	2	1	3	8	6	2	2	1	2					27
7	0	4	1	4	3	1	4	1	1					19
8	1	1	0	1	3	0	0	1	0	1	2			10
9	2	1	2	0	0	0	2	0	2					9
10	1	1	0	0	0	2	1	0	1	1				7
11	1	0	0	1	0	2	0	1	1	0	2			8
12	1	0	1	0	0	0	2	2						6
SE*	0	0	1	2	0	0	0	2						5
Total	101	112	104	69	41	20	18	8	7	2	4	0	0	486

*Nongraded special education class.
Chart indicates that fifty-two kindergarten students spent between thirteen and thirty-six months classified speech impaired.

CHART 12.6B The Number of Months Students in District 9 Had Been Classified Speech Impaired (by grade by number of students).

Grade	Number of Months													Total
	12	24	36	48	60	72	84	96	108	120	132	144	156	
K	1	6	9											16
1	5	1	11	4										21
2	4	1	1	1	1									8
3	1	3	1	4	6	2								17
4	4			2	3									9
5								1						1
6														0
7														0
8														0
9														0
10														0
11														0
12														0
Total	15	11	22	11	10	2	0	1	0	0	0	0	0	72

Chart indicates that nine kindergarten students spent between twenty-five and thirty-six months classified speech impaired.

are there so many students not classified SI in District 6 receiving speech therapy? Are these speech programs well managed and supervised? Are these effective and efficient operations? Could these students be assisted as well in all day general classes with or without the help of consultants as they are in general classes for most of the day and speech therapy for two to five times a week? What would be the savings if students could be serviced equally well in general classes by consultants? What would you do with the 60% to 100% of your speech therapists that provide pull-out services?

NUMBER OF SI TEACHERS

My special education audits of different districts indicate that your resource room teachers/speech therapists probably account for 50% of the time special education staff spend with SI students. You understand that a reduction in the number of SI students means that you can reduce the number of resource room teachers/speech therapists or use these staff members in some more effective manner. Some of these resource room teachers/speech therapists can be used as consul-

tants and serve a larger number of students and general education teachers than they do in the present structure of special education. You can determine the degree to which you can downsize this portion of your SI program and the amount of money you are able to save and still deliver a quality special education program.

CRITICISMS OF PULL-OUT SPEECH THERAPY PROGRAMS

You need to be aware of criticisms of pull-out speech therapy programs if you are going to deal with these issues. Dr. Nancy A. Creaghead, chair, department of communication sciences and disorders at the University of Cincinnati, noted the concerns of people in the speech field who oppose pull-out programs and favor collaboration and consultation models of speech language therapy. Dr. Creaghead (1990) wrote:

> Special needs children should be served within the classroom environment. Consider the learning disabled child who leaves his or her class for speech therapy, for remedial reading, for LD resource room, and for counseling. This child is put at a disadvantage

CHART 12.7 Number of Months Students in District 8 Are Classified SI (by ethnicity/race).

Ethnicity/Race	Average Number of Months	Percent of Students Classified LD at Least 60 Months	Percent of Students That Moved or Dropped out of School
White	31	12	8
Hispanic	37	16	20
African American	17	0	30

in several ways. First, when she or he is absent from class, she or he misses some of the script information present in the classroom—especially the information that is given at transition times. . . . Second, this child with special needs must learn a number of scripts that the "normal" children do not have to learn. Third, this child, who has already shown that she or he has difficulty generalizing experiences to acquire the scripts of the classroom, is asked to learn new information in one script (e.g., speech therapy) and transfer this information to a different script in the classroom. For example, in speech therapy, she or he may work on following directions when they are provided explicitly in a one-to-one context. . . . In the classroom, directions may be implicit and given to the whole group. In summary not only is this child missing classroom script information and being asked to learn additional scripts, she or he is also asked to figure out how learning acquired in one context applies to a different context. When these factors are considered, it is not surprising that we have failed to help some children succeed in school.

EMOTIONALLY DISTURBED

In the course of my special education audits, I have analyzed districts that have between 5% and 12% of classified students classified ED. Districts 10 and 11 differ in the percent of ED students that have been classified for less than five years. Charts 12.8A and 12.8B indicate that between 77% and 97% of students classified ED have been classified for less than five years. On the other hand, between 3% and 23% of students have been classified for more than five years.

You need to know why these ED students have been classified for more than five years. How long should the program take to effect change in mildly to moderately handicapped ED students' behavior and coping skills? And you need to know whether race/ethnicity enter into the equation of students classified ED.

LENGTH OF TIME STUDENTS ARE CLASSIFIED ED BY ETHNICITY/RACE

Although the information on ethnicity/race of students classified ED from my special education audit of District 10 cannot be generalized, it does show you how to determine whether there might be subtle problems inherent in the ED program. Chart 12.9 indicates that, although white students tend to be classified ED for a longer period of time than Latino and African American students, this picture would change drastically if ED minority students did not move and/or drop out of school at a higher rate than ED white students.

ED STUDENTS WHO RECEIVE REGULAR CLASSROOM INSTRUCTION AND RELATED SERVICES OR RESOURCE ROOM OR PART-TIME SPECIAL CLASS PROGRAMS AND ED STUDENTS ENROLLED IN SPECIAL PUBLIC SCHOOLS OR NONSCHOOL FACILITIES

You need to factor in the percent of ED students that receive related services and the percent of ED students enrolled in special facilities in order to get a true picture

CHART 12.8A **The Number of Months Students in District 10 Have Been Classified Emotionally Disturbed (by grade by number of students).**

Grade	12	24	36	48	60	72	84	96	108	120	132	144	156	Total
K	6	3												9
1	1	1	3											5
2	2	5	3	4	2	1								17
3	4	1	2	1	3	1								12
4	3	2	3	4	1	1								14
5	3	2	3	1	3	3								15
6	4	1	6	1	2	1	2	1						18
7	3	2	6	3	4	1	0	3						22
8	7	5	2	5	2	5	2							28
9	10	3	4	4	3	0	1	4	0	1				30
10	5	3	3	0	1	1	3	3						19
11	8	0	1	4	0	1	5	1	0	1	2	0	1	24
12	2	5	1	5	4	2	0	3	1	1	1	0	1	26
SE*	3	11	7	8	5	1	2	3	1	1	1	0	1	44
Total	61	44	44	40	30	18	15	18	2	4	4	0	3	283

*Nongraded special education class.
Chart indicates that six kindergarten students spent between one and twelve months classified emotionally disturbed.

CHART 12.8B The Number of Months Students in District 11 Have Been Classified Emotionally Disturbed (by grade by number of students).

						Number of Months								
Grade	12	24	36	48	60	72	84	96	108	120	132	144	156	Total
K	5													5
1		1												1
2			1											1
3														0
4	1	1												2
5		1		1										2
6	3	1	2											6
7		1												1
8														0
9	1			1										2
10		1	1		1									3
11					2									2
12		1	1	3		1								6
Total	10	7	5	5	3	1	0	0	0	0	0	0	0	31

Chart indicates that five kindergarten students spent between one and twelve months classified emotionally disturbed.

of your ED program. Approximately 21% of classified students classified ED receive regular classroom instruction and related services, and approximately 18% of students enrolled in special public schools or centers for the handicapped and special education provided in home, hospital, or other nonschool facility are classified emotionally disturbed. In District 11, 26% of ED students receive regular classroom instruction and related services, and 32% of students enrolled in special public schools or centers for the handicapped and special education provided in home, hospital, or other nonschool facility are classified emotionally disturbed. If you are in District 11, you want to know the reasons that you have a larger percent of ED students in regular classes that receive related services, and you want to know whether the number of students in special schools is so small that an increase or decrease in one or two students distorts percentages.

ED STUDENTS IN PULL-OUT PROGRAMS: AN EXAMPLE

I have found that the number and percent of ED students in pull-out is considerably less than the number and percent of LD and SI students. In District 11, ten

out of thirty-one (32%) students classified emotionally disturbed, grades K–12, received regular classroom instruction and related services or resource room or part-time special class programs. The number of students by grade was

Grade	Number of Students
K	0
1	0
2	0
3	0
4	1
5	0
6	0
7	0
8	0
9	0
10	2
11	3
12	4
	10

When I saw these data, I was curious to know the

CHART 12.9 Number of Months Students in District 10 Are Classified ED (by ethnicity/race).

Ethnicity/Race	Average Number of Months	Percent of Students Classified LD at Least 60 Months	Percent of Students That Moved or Dropped out of School
White	41	24	16
Hispanic	29	20	20
African American	15	0	32

CHART 12.10 Percent of Students Classified LD, SI, and ED (by ethnicity/race).

	Ethnic/Racial Enrollment District	Percent of Classified Students	Percent of LD Students	Percent of SI Students	Percent of ED Students
African American	1.1%	2.1%	1.5	2.0	3.4
Hispanic	3.1%	4.5%	4.5	5.2	5.2
White	93.7%	92.4%	92.4	88.6	88.4

reasons that high school students made up 90% of the pull-out program for ED students. Are these high school students in true pull-out programs, or is a period scheduled into the student's day? How many of your elementary ED students are in pull-out programs? Would they benefit more by remaining in general classes all day? After all, do most or some of these students have problems focusing and dealing with change and authority?

NUMBER OF ED TEACHERS

My special education audits of different districts indicate that your resource room teachers probably account for 3% of the time special education staff spend with ED students. You understand that a reduction in the number of ED students means that you can reduce the number of resource room teachers or that you can use these staff members in some more effective manner. Some of these resource room teachers can be used as consultants and serve a larger number of students and general education teachers than they do in the present structure of special education. You can determine the degree to which you can downsize this portion of your ED program and the amount of money you are able to save and still deliver a quality special education program.

FIFTH STEP TO DOWNSIZE THE NUMBER OF CLASSIFIED STUDENTS BY CATEGORIES

MINORITY STUDENTS

You need to keep in mind the concerns that may exist in your community that special education is an "alter-

native program" for minority students and perhaps poor white students. Charts 12.10 and 12.11 provide you with pictures of District 12 that point out the subtleties that oftentimes are missed or minimized about the ethnic/racial makeup of your special education program. Chart 12.10 indicates that the percent of minority classified students in District 12 exceed the percent of minority students in the district. This was more pronounced for ED students. However, Chart 12.11 indicates that when the number of students by category is compared to the total number of classified students from the same ethnic/racial group the placement of students is questionable and warrants attention. In other words, how do you explain the percent of all African American classified students who are classified ED? Is the placement of students within the LD and ED categories linked to the ethnic/racial background of students?

SUMMARY

This chapter walks you through a process that helps you build accountability into your special education program and shows you step by step how to downsize and reduce special education costs in an educationally sound, ethical, and methodical manner. You are sensitized to the relationship between the length of time students are classified and the costs of your special education program. You are encouraged to question the rationale for any LD, SI, and ED students classified for five years. You are shown educational and cost benefits that accrue to students and your district by minimizing and/or eliminating pull-out programs, especially for LD and SI students. Finally, you have a model to use to make sure that ethnicity/race is minimized as a factor

CHART 12.11 Percent of Each Ethnic/Racial Group That Is Classified LD, SI, or ED.

	Ethnic/Racial Enrollment District	Percent of LD Students	Percent of SI Students	Percent of ED Students
African American	1.1%	37.2	19.6	17.6
Hispanic	3.1%	49.5	23.0	13.2
White	93.7%	53.3	20.6	11.9

in the placement of students within the LD, SI, and ED categories in your district. This chapter helps you ensure that you have an accountable program, one that is educationally sound, concerned about students, ethical, and yet effective and efficient.

REFERENCE

Creaghead, N. (1990). Mutual Empowerment through Collaboration: A New Script for an Old Problem, *Best Practices in School Speech Language Pathology,* 1:109–116.

13

The Declassification Process

AIM

THE purpose of this chapter is to describe the declassification process and help you overcome three bottlenecks that hinder an equitable, objective, and effective declassification process. The three bottlenecks that limit the effectiveness of the declassification process include (1) the lack of written criteria for declassification of students, (2) concerns and fears that declassified students will lower schoolwide test scores, and (3) gender and ethnic/racial bias. This chapter points out the problems in the declassification process caused by the lack of written criteria for the declassification of LD, SI, and ED students. It sensitizes you to misconceptions held by psychologists, special education teachers, and CSE members about the existence of written criteria for declassification. You are provided with a list of criteria to help you put your own written criteria in place in your district. There are charts to illustrate patterns and concerns with the declassification process. This chapter walks you through steps to determine whether the failure to declassify students is linked to concerns and fears about schoolwide test scores, gender, and/or ethnicity/race.

INTRODUCTION

There are five facts that I gathered from my special education audits that point out problems with the declassification process and should help you focus your thoughts on steps to improve the declassification process:

- First, you need to know that very few students are declassified. My special education audits indicate that approximately 2% to 5% of classified students are declassified each year. The 2% to 5% does not include students who graduate, move, or drop out of school. It only includes those students that are declassified.
- Second, you need to know that the bulk of students declassified had been classified SI. Of this 2% to 5%, approximately 74% of them had been classified SI. The other 26% includes students classified LD, ED, and/or OHI.
- Third, nearly 88% of students declassified are in elementary school (K–6).
- Fourth, approximately 62% of declassified students are males and 38% of declassified students are females. However, the percentage of males declassified is usually smaller than the percentage of males referred for evaluation for placement in special education. The percentage of females declassified is larger than the percent of females referred for evaluation for placement in special education.
- Fifth, the average declassified student has been classified between thirty and forty-nine months.

Surely, you realize that these figures indicate that the size of your special education program will continue to grow by leaps and bounds if more students are not declassified, and most certainly, older students will tend to be institutionalized into the program. After all, only 12% of declassified students are in secondary school. You can also expect the small number of students who are declassified to be in the program between two and a half and four years. The special education program will continue to be a male club. Most importantly, you cannot expect to make a dent in the size of your LD and ED populations if the current rate of declassification continues. In order to turn the tide, you need to make sure that the declassification process in place is equitable, objective, and effective.

BOTTLENECK 1: LACK OF WRITTEN CRITERIA FOR DECLASSIFICATION

DIRECTOR OF SPECIAL EDUCATION

You need to know that there is a great deal of confusion among special education personnel regarding the existence of written criteria for the declassification of students in their district. In every special education audit that I conduct, I find that directors of special education report that there are not written criteria in place for the declassification of LD and ED students from special education:

- Occasionally, there are criteria in place for the declassification of SI students.
- Sometimes, directors of special education report that criteria for declassification of SI, LD, and ED students are being developed.
- Some psychologists, special education teachers, CSE members, and principals report that they have not seen any written declassification criteria for LD and ED students.
- There is a greater percentage of psychologists, followed by special education teachers, CSE members, and principals, who indicate that their district has written criteria for the declassification of LD and ED students.

You need to be sure that your psychologists, special education teachers, and CSE members are not observing an eleventh commandment and covering up problems in the declassification process. After all, how could these highly educated professionals mistake the existence of a written criteria for declassification of youngsters when one does not exist? How do these people make objective and consistent decisions when written criteria to declassify are not in place? And how much of a bottleneck is the lack of written criteria to the declassification of students?

DECLASSIFICATION OF SI STUDENTS

You are more likely to find that your district has written criteria in place for the declassification of SI students than LD or ED students. My special education audits indicate that, occasionally, there are written criteria in place for declassification of SI students. Some principals and special education teachers report that they rely on the opinion of the speech pathologist/teacher to make a decision on whether a student should be declassified SI. According to principals, special education teachers, and CSE members, students are declassified SI:

- who no longer score below the 25th percentile on two or more subtests of formal testing and who are able to function successfully in the classroom
- who score in the average range
- when they improve in language skills so that there is less than a one year discrepancy
- when they are able to function in the mainstream program
- when their skills problems improve
- when therapy is no longer beneficial
- when their disabilities are remedied

Do principals and special education teachers in your district rely solely on the opinion of the speech pathologist/teacher to make declassification decisions? Does your district have written criteria in place for the declassification of SI students? If so, do the criteria value both quantitative and qualitative information?

DECLASSIFICATION OF LD STUDENTS

There are a range of comments made by psychologists, special education teachers, CSE members, and principals that point out their erroneous perceptions about the existence of written criteria for the declassification of LD students; however, their answers point out that they believe that the state criteria for classification of youngsters, student abilities as evaluated by tests and observations, and student success in mainstream programs without the need for support services should be considered as criteria for declassification. Following are a range of comments that you can expect to hear from your psychologists, special education teachers, CSE members, and principals on the written declassification criteria in place in your district.

STATE CRITERIA AND/OR A 50% DISCREPANCY

- Declassification uses the same criteria as classification. When students no longer meet criteria for classification, they are declassified.
- If students no longer require services according to state guidelines and actual classroom functioning, they are declassified.
- Students no longer met the criteria for classification or the criteria outlined in state regulations or the 50% discrepancy level.
- The written criteria for declassification of students from special education was either "state mandate" or that the student no longer met the criteria for classification or the student no longer met the 50% discrepancy guidelines.

TEST AND OBSERVATION

- The criteria include the results of educational testing, teacher reports, observations of students, and the student's ability to organize himself/herself, be responsible for his/her work, and be socially appropriate.
- Declassification depends on testing, class performance, and a team decision.
- Students are declassified when they show significant improvement in classwork and on annual and triennial assessments and improvement on standardized tests.
- Teacher evaluates student's academic performance, growth, and success.
- Student achieves independently at their grade level or their highest level of achievement.
- Student's performance levels on diagnostic, standardized, and classroom tests, as well as daily performance, increase to the point where the teacher can fully expect continued improvement.
- The criteria include marked improvement in standardized test scores, academic progress proportional to standardized scores, and the student's display of success independent of support services.
- On a case by case basis, the committee evaluates the reports and student performance. When appropriate, children are declassified.

SUCCESS IN MAINSTREAMED CLASSES WITHOUT THE NEED OF SUPPORT SERVICES

- Students are to be considered for declassification when they have shown success in the mainstream to a degree that the building team feels they can make it (pass) without services.
- The student has successfully participated in a mainstream program for a reasonable amount of time.
- Students can function in mainstream programs and meet IEP goals.
- Students have experienced six months of successful mainstreaming.
- There have been recent educational evaluations and/or a psychological assessment to determine the level of achievement of a student in the mainstream program and the degree to which the handicapping condition interferes with learning.
- The child is put on transitional support services (TSS) for a specified period of time by a chairman's report or CSE and a return to CSE

to evaluate before declassification.
- When a student is able to successfully complete grade level requirements without any support services, he/she is declassified.
- When a child reaches his or her potential in an area of special learning and is found to have progressed and continues to move ahead without the need for special help, he/she is declassified.
- When it has been determined, based on the reports and test results presented by the building team, that the student has improved to the point of no longer needing services, he is declassified.

Your psychologists, special education teachers, CSE members, and principals can provide you with a wealth of information needed to develop criteria for the declassification of LD students. Tap into their collective knowledge. What type of role do you want general education teachers and parents of special education students to have in the declassification process? What type of information can general education teachers and parents of special education students provide to better ensure the success of declassified youngsters?

DECLASSIFICATION OF ED STUDENTS

There are a range of comments made by psychologists, special education teachers, CSE members, and principals that point out their erroneous perceptions about the existence of written criteria for the declassification of ED students; however, their answers shed light on abilities and behaviors that need to be considered when you put criteria in place in your district to declassify ED students. Here are a range of comments that you can expect to hear from your psychologists, special education teachers, CSE members, and principals on the written declassification criteria for ED students in place in your district. ED students are declassified when they (their)

- function within two years of their grade level and are recommended by their teachers
- are able to perform in a regular setting
- are able to manage their emotional problems
- behavior does not interfere with their academic performance
- maintain socially appropriate behaviors with peers and faculty
- function successfully without a restrictive environment

You need to work with your professional staff to develop criteria for the declassification of ED students.

Do you want parents of special education students to play a role in the declassification process? What information can parents of special education students provide to better ensure the success of declassified ED students?

ACTUAL REASONS FOR DECLASSIFICATION OF STUDENTS

You might be interested in my findings from one district about actual reasons that are given by the CSE to declassify students. Please notice that the terms are not measurable but are vague and nebulous. There is not an operational definition of "improved" or "test grades." How do you evaluate the credibility of "teacher recommendations"? There is no way to ensure yourself that another CSE would declassify students with the same information in hand. In other words, the declassification process appears to be mysterious to outsiders. For instance, in this district, 64% of general classroom teachers and 47% of parents are ignorant of the workings of the declassification process. What is more alarming is that 65% of parents who have youngsters in special education for at least five years do not know how students get declassified. Is it any wonder that general classroom teachers worry about the success of declassified students placed in their classes? Is there any wonder that the credibility of the special education program is continually suspect? The most frequent reasons for declassification, in descending order, are

- teacher recommendations
- improved/adequate grades
- report card grades
- improved articulation
- improved expressive language
- academic performance
- test grades

Do you know the reasons that students are declassified in your district? Are the criteria for declassification well defined? Do general education teachers and parents of special education students have a role to play in the development of declassification criteria? Have you explained the criteria to general education classroom teachers and parents? Do you need to inservice principals, general education teachers, special education teachers, psychologists, and CSE members about the criteria for declassification of students? Do you know the role that principals and special education personnel have in the declassification process?

ROLES OF PRINCIPALS IN THE DECLASSIFICATION PROCESS

We all know that principals are regarded as key figures in the success of general education programs,

but we need to know the role principals have in the declassification process. As a result of my special education audits, I find that principals view their role as managers in the declassification process. The terms and statements they use to describe their role include

- Set tone not to classify students merely because they are a behavioral problem.
- Work with staff, educate parents and students, and encourage parents to follow CSE recommendations.
- Interact with CSE.
- Establish building team agenda.
- Run building meeting smoothly, take care of paperwork, analyze information, and make recommendations to the CSE.
- Facilitate management of policies and time lines; get necessary information to the building committee.
- Interpret data for building committee.
- Recommend classification or declassification and vote.
- Make sure data were summarized accurately; knowledge of the law.
- Review programs that my building can offer other than special education for students.

Are these the roles you think principals ought to have in the declassification process in your school/district? Are the abilities and skills of principals underutilized in the declassification process? What knowledge and skills would they need to have more than a managerial role in the declassification process and make the declassification process more accountable? How do principals make recommendations when they do not know the criteria for declassification? Would the percent of students declassified increase if principals were more knowledgeable about the operations of special education? Would there be an increase in declassifications if principals were made more accountable for special education students and programs in their buildings?

ROLE OF SPECIAL EDUCATION PERSONNEL IN THE DECLASSIFICATION PROCESS

Special education personnel see themselves as key people in decisions to declassify youngsters. They have both the quantitative and qualitative information needed to make decisions. They state that they

- Review test data, teacher reports, and report cards.
- Read and interpret scores and present the case.
- Make recommendations regarding student's

academic, emotional, and additional performance.
- Evaluate student's ability to handle general education programs without special education services.

There is no doubt that special education personnel are key players in decisions to declassify students. By the way, when I survey and interview parents, I find that approximately 65% of parents who have youngsters in special education for at least five years think that special education teachers are very significant in the declassification process. What role do special education personnel have in the declassification process in your school/district? Are their roles spelled out in a job description? How do they reach consistent decisions if your school/district lacks written criteria for declassification of students?

STEPS TO BUILD EQUITY, OBJECTIVITY, AND ACCOUNTABILITY INTO THE DECLASSIFICATION PROCESS

In order to ensure the equity, objectivity, and effectiveness of the declassification process, you need to develop written criteria. The criteria should be used to determine whether students are declassified—not the fears and whims of principals and/or general education teachers. Somewhere, many years ago, I came across a list of criteria for declassifying students. Unfortunately, I cannot locate the citation. The list mirrored the insights provided by special education teachers, principals, and CSE members in my audits. The criteria for declassification of students requires that you quantify, when possible, students' abilities to

- function at or near the average of the mainstreamed class
- use regular class materials such as textbooks and worksheets
- perform consistency
- work independently
- adjust to delays
- follow directions
- follow classroom routine
- work in close proximity to others

BOTTLENECK 2: CONCERNS/FEARS ABOUT SCHOOLWIDE TEST SCORES

ILLUSTRATION: DECLASSIFICATION OF STUDENTS BY GRADE

District 13 declassified 5% of special education students. Chart 13.1 helps to clarify the declassification

trends in District 13 for the school community. Chart 13.1 points out that the percent of females declassified decreases from elementary to secondary school. Also, Chart 13.1 shows that, in District 13, the declassification rate is low in grade 3, a grade in which there is a great deal of formal testing of students. The rate of declassification is low in transitional grades 6 and 8 and in high school grades 10, 11, and 12.

What declassification patterns would you find in your district if you developed Chart 13.1? Are third graders not declassified because general classroom teachers and elementary principals are worried that the declassified students would lower class and schoolwide test scores? Or are they not declassified because the third grade is traditionally the grade in which students are asked for the first time to use reading and mathematics skills to learn other content areas? And if this is so, when will the system declassify these students?

BOTTLENECK 3: GENDER AND ETHNIC/RACIAL BIAS

ILLUSTRATION: DEMOGRAPHICS OF DECLASSIFIED STUDENTS

District 14 has a district enrollment of approximately 3100 students. Chart 13.2 indicates the demographics related to declassified students in District 14. Two percent of classified students were declassified. Although you cannot generalize from these data, you can see that these students, who had been in the program for an average of forty-nine months, tend to be in elementary school, tend to be classified SI, and are mainly males. How does this picture compare with the actual situation in your district? If your district mirrors that of District 14 what steps can you take to change the situation?

DECLASSIFICATION OF MINORITY STUDENTS

You need to review declassification data carefully, especially as you analyze ethnic/racial patterns. For instance, in Chart 13.3, you need only look at the relationship between the percentage of each ethnic/racial group in the district, students referred for evaluation for placement in special education, and students declassified to see the problems facing District 15. Does ethnicity/race play a role in declassification decisions in your district? If so, what steps can you take to change this situation? Do you need to brainstorm with and inservice your principals, general education teachers, special education teachers, psychologists, and CSE members about ethnic/racial patterns in the declassification of students?

Chart 13.4 indicates that, in District 16, white students are the largest group declassified. However, only

CHART 13.1 Declassification of Students by Grade by Gender in District 13.

Grade	Number of Students Declassified	Number of Males Declassified	Number of Females Declassified	Percent of Students Declassified
1	7	5	2	10.1
2	8	7	1	11.6
3	5	3	2	7.2
4	11	4	7	15.9
5	7	3	4	10.1
6	4	3	1	5.8
7	8	2	6	11.6
8	2	1	1	2.9
9	8	7	1	11.6
10	1	1	0	1.4
11	5	5	0	7.2
12	3	3	0	4.3

CHART 13.2 Number of Students in District 14 Declassified by Gender, Grade, Classification, and Length of Time Classified.

Gender	Grade	Classification	Months
M	3	SI	18
M	3	SI	54
M	3	SI	37
F	K	SI	30
F	4	LD	7
F	K	SI	27
M	5	SI	87
M	9	ED	48

CHART 13.3 Percent of Total Enrollment, Referrals, and Declassification by Ethnic/Racial Groups in District 15.

	Percent of Total Enrollment	Percent of Referrals	Percent of Students Declassified
Black	12	17	10
Hispanic	4	8	1
White	84	75	89

CHART 13.4 Percent of Students Declassified by Ethnic/Racial Group in District 15.

	Percent of All Students Declassified	Percent of Each Ethnicity/ Race Declassified
Black	2.4	1.7
Hispanic	4.8	1.7
White	90.2	1.9

1.9% of all classified white students are declassified. No matter how you look at this data, it is clear that a very small number of minority students are declassified. They make up a small percentage of all students declassified, and they make up an even smaller percentage of the total special education minority population that is declassified.

SUMMARY

You now know the steps you need to take to improve the declassification process. You know the abilities and behaviors to consider in the writing of criteria for your school/district. You need to plan, implement, and evaluate inservice programs for principals, general education teachers, special education teachers, psychologists, CSE members, and parents to have a successful declassification process. And you know how to organize data so that you can make a reasonable determination as to whether the failure to declassify students is linked to concerns about schoolwide test scores, gender, and/or ethnicity/race. Once you address these issues, you are well on your way to eliminating bottlenecks that hinder the declassification process and downsizing special education.

14

Conclusion

THERE is no doubt that, if you use the process spelled out in this book and the included forms and charts and digest and apply the wealth of information crammed into each chapter, you will improve the way your special education program does business. Your special education program becomes more equitable, objective, and effective. You remove the fat in your special education program; reduce the referrals and classification of large numbers of males, minorities, and poor youngsters; and improve the quality of education you deliver to classified students. Only students who need to be classified will be in special education programs. No longer will youngsters be classified because they are a pain in someone's neck, nor will youngsters be classified because the general education curriculum is not developmentally appropriate. Nor will students remain classified for years and years, and you will downsize and reduce the cost of your special education program.

This step-by-step approach, coupled with survey forms and charts, helps you to unscramble the special education puzzle and shows you and others how each piece of the puzzle affects the integrity, size, and cost of special education. Throughout each chapter, the implications of your likely findings are discussed.

If you make an oral presentation to either a board of education or to a specific group such as general education teachers or psychologists, just select the appropriate charts for your presentation. For instance, when you speak to general education teachers, you might want to show them Charts 4.1 to 9.7. When you debrief psychologists, you might want to share with them the responses from general education teachers, principals, and CSE members. Also, you might want their thoughts about the intelligence range of students by classification categories. Let me suggest that, whenever possible, let the data speak for itself. Place your charts on an overhead projector, show them to your audience, and explain the charts just to be sure the audience understands fully what they see. Ask your audience to interpret the data. Listen, and be prepared to ask questions about their interpretations. Finally, elicit recommendations on how to improve parts of the process discussed.

The format in this book is arranged so that you can write a formative or summative report about each part of the special education process. The charts and explanations for the referral process, classification process, and declassification process are in the order needed for a report. Just add your data, and you have a customized report. The details of the report contain a wealth of information about your district specifically, and that is the value of your report.

The information is this book is arranged so that you can deal with one aspect or all aspects of the special education program. You can improve the referral process this year or you can improve the referral process and declassification process. You know the demands you face and the resources available to you. Once again, good luck.

Index

Academic underachievement, 41–44 (*see* Low achieving students)

Acronyms/terms, 1, 2, 41–42, 52, 59–60, 76, 80–83

African-American, 25, 70, 73–75, 79, 122 (*see* Minority students)

ALGOZZINE, 41, 47

Annual reviews, 25

Anonymity/confidentiality, 6, 27

Assessment data, 68, 119

Audits, 1, 3, 5, 23, 27, 95, 101, 103

BASIS Achievement Test, 68 (*see* Assessment data)

Bender-Gestalt, 68 (*see* Assessment data)

Berry Development Test of Visual Motor Inventory, 68 (*see* Assessment data)

Board of education, 21, 25

Boilerplate reports, 24, 29, 33, 35

CELF-R, 68

Classification
length of time, 103–113
process, 66–67

Classroom teachers, 8, 26, 27, 57, 66, 68

CMT: FOR TEACHERS (*see* Software)

Committee on Special Education (CSE), 14, 65–71

Connor Rating Scale, 65

Consultant models, 109

CRAIGHEAD, N., 101, 111, 115

CREVT, 68 (*see* Assessment data)

CSE chairperson, 1, 3, 66

CSE members, 5, 11, 14, 15, 18, 27, 30, 66

Curriculum alignment, 95

Curriculum guides, 6, 21, 33, 95–98

Curriculum and instruction, 44, 46, 95–101

Curriculum mapping, 99–100

Database boilerplates, 5, 7, 28

Database file, 5, 7

Declassification, 117–123

Director of Special Education, 69, 85, 89, 93, 118, 120

Educational evaluator, 66

Emotionally disturbed (ED), 53, 57–63, 112, 119

Equity, 27, 35

Ethnic/race, 21, 27, 70, 107

Family status, 27, 35–38, 46, 54, 63

Females (*see* Gender)

FIGUEROA, R., 21, 43, 47

Foster household (*see* Family status)

GARTNER, 39, 47

Gender, 21, 27, 29, 33, 41–42, 44, 51–53, 58–59, 68, 71, 74–75, 78–79, 122

Guidance counselors, 21

Health curriculum, 100

Human resources, 23–25

IEP objectives, 6, 96, 98–99

Instruments to conduct audit, 5

Intelligence, 42–44, 54, 61–62, 69

Job descriptions, 6

Latino students, 70, 74, 79, 82–83, 107 (*see* Minority students)

LD teacher consultants, 92–93, 109

Learning disabled (LD), 39–47, 53, 106–107, 118

LIPSKY, 39, 47

Low achieving students, 40, 42–43

Mainstreaming, 105–106

Males (*see* Gender)

McGUE, 41, 47

Medical model, 43

Minority students/ethnicity, 73–83, 107, 110, 112, 114, 121–122 (*see* African-American, Ethnic/race, and Latino students)

Nuclear family (*see* Family status)

Parents/guardians, 1, 3, 5–6, 18–21, 27, 66, 101

Peabody Picture Vocabulary Test–Revised (PPVT-R), 68 (*see* Assessment data)

Placement of students, 22

Pre-schoolers, 46, 49, 59

Prereferrals, 3

Primary grades, 44, 49, 53

Principals, 1, 3, 5, 15–16, 21–22, 27, 30, 32, 66, 86–91, 120

Psychologists, 5–6, 11–12, 21, 27, 30, 32, 42–43, 65–67, 92–93

Pull-out programs, 108, 110–114, 119

Referrals, 3, 21, 25, 27–37, 42, 50

Remediate problems, 27, 31

Resource room, part-time programs (*see* Pull-out programs)

ROWVT, 68 (*see* Assessment data)

Stanford Binet, 68 (*see* Assessment data)

Secondary schools, 61

Single parent family (*see* Family status)

Size of special education program, 23

SLINN, 41, 47

Special education personnel, 5, 7, 9, 21, 25, 27, 30–32, 66, 85–93, 109, 120

Special education task force (SETF), 5, 21–25

Special public day school, 6

Speech impaired (SI), 41, 49–56, 110–111, 118

Social studies audits, 96–97

Social workers, 21, 66, 92–93

Socio-economic status, 6

Software (CMT: FOR TEACHERS), 95–96

Speech therapist, 21, 53, 66

State education department, 6, 23–25

State officials, 3

Summative reports, 22–25, 27, 29, 33, 35, 39

Survey forms, 5–9, 11–12, 14–16, 18–20

TAT, 68 (*see* Assessment data)
Teacher comments/terms
    academic, 41–42, 76
    behavioral, 41, 59–60, 76–77
    other, 41, 77

speech and language, 41, 51–52, 77
Teaching assistants, 6, 90–91
TOLD, 69 (*see* Assessment data)
Transfer students, 29, 44, 51
Triennial review, 25

WISC III, 68 (*see* Assessment data)
WISC-R, 68 (*see* Assessment data)
WLPB, 68 (*see* Assessment data)

YESSELDYKE, 41, 47

About the Author

DONALD F. WEINSTEIN, President and founder of Educational Services Associates, Inc., has worked as a supervisor of middle schools, principal, district director of curriculum, administrative assistant for research and development and curriculum and instruction, and associate professor of educational administration. As a result of his vision and experience he has improved the management and operation of special education programs. Dr. Weinstein designed, planned, and implemented creative and sound approaches to ensure the equity, objectivity, and effectiveness of the referral, classification, and declassification processes. As a result, districts were able to take systematic steps to downsize special education, reduce costs, and ensure the proper placement of students and better delivery of instruction.

Dr. Weinstein designed and implemented audits of the management and operation of special education programs for public school districts and intermediate units. He evaluated the linkage between curriculum goals/objectives and special education IEP objectives and criterion. He gave workshops on the referral, classification, and declassification processes. Dr. Weinstein designed, implemented, and evaluated the delivery of education programs to both mainstream and special education classes. He served on a special education evaluation accreditation team. Dr. Weinstein analyzed the cost of sending special education students to regional education units for services. He audited small and large special education programs, programs that had as many as 2500 classified students. He has published numerous articles on special education. Dr. Weinstein has presented his research on the referral, classification, and declassification processes and racial/ethnic and gender issues at professional conferences.